In The Midst of CHAOS:

MANIFESTING
Life Through Co-Creation

By:
#1 International Bestselling Author
Zachary Shiloh Watts

ELITE PUBLISHING
HOUSE
YOUR LEGACY. YOUR BOOK.

First Edition

Copyright 2023 © Zachary Shiloh Watts

All Rights Reserved

No part of this book may be reproduced or transmitted in any form or by any means, electronical or mechanical, including photocopying, recording or by an information storage an retrieval system – except by a reviewer who may quote brie passages in a review to be printed in a magazine, newspaper or on the Web – without permission in writing from the publisher.

Cover Graphics: Kathryn Denhof

This is dedicated to all of you out there. The kids out there. When I say kids, I mean adults who bought this book.

The struggling business owner.

The person who works a day-to-day job.

Anyone who is scared of uncertainty.

All who scrap to get by.

Overweight who are on weight loss journeys.

Diabetics who yearn to be diabetes free.

People who want to reduce their medical prescription drug use.

Individuals who moved back in (with their biological families) after months (or years) of being away.

Caretakers

Nerds who were told that being nerdy won't make you successful.

The storytellers who have stories to share.

The people hurting, who are seeking multidimensional healing.

To quote Kermit the Frog, "The lovers, dreamers, and me."

Warning

Reader discretion is advised. Some people are offended by colorful language. If cussing bothers you, then you were warned (in advance).

What you are about to read is by the author. All of the content in this book is his stories, memories, and podcast content. They reflect his reality.

Table of Contents

Thank You *8*

Welcome *10*

Fall 2019 & Journal Writing *12*

BLK Lion's Roar (Solo Version) *14*

Zachary Shiloh Blacks Out *15*

Universal Laws *16*

She Is Magic & DreamBuilder *18*

They Are Magic *21*

Beginning My Survival in a Retail Jungle *28*

Wolverine vs Sabretooth (Becoming A Leader then Manifesting My Greatest Workplace Foe) *31*

Letters of Magic *34*

Ascension Visionary Leaders *42*

Huns, Kins, and Loves *47*

Letters of Love II *50*

Zachary Shiloh's Letter to Michelle Obama......................56

The BLK Lion's Roars Become Disorganized 58

Magical Miracles 59

Rebel Romance... 64

Dare To Dream 70

Zachary Shiloh is Overcome by Overwhelm...................... 74

Being A Best-Selling Author 77

Why Co-Author? 84

Going Solo 85

Mind Over Matter Unlimited 88

Partners In Believing 92

Taking Chances, Making Mistakes, and Getting Messy 95

Cold Showers 97

Inner Child.. 99

Shadow Work 102

Intermittent Fasting/My Abundance 107

Exercise... 113

Meditation 121

Staying Consistent *130*

Being Truthful *133*

Knowing My Worth *135*

Not Giving Up *138*

Blessing What I Do Have / Not Giving Up Part II............ *141*

GSD (Getting Shit Done) *144*

Having Fun *147*

What Zachary Shiloh Eats to Stay Under 200 Pounds *152*

The Forbidden *158*

The Untouchables *162*

Where Am I Now *165*

Outro *166*

About the Author *168*

Thank You

God:

For being the almighty source that breathes me. Communicating with me multi-dimensionally. Never leaving or truly forsaking me.

My biological family/non-writing friends:

For inspiring me to better myself.

Elite Publishing House:

My main home in the writing world. This is our fifth go-together. Every time we have worked together, it has manifested gold.

DarkQuarks Publishing:

My second writing home. Allowing me to be more myself. Pushing me out of my comfort zone.

Melissa Desveaux:

The first solo international Publisher I worked with.

To my co-authors:

For their time, talent, and energy put into our books.

All of the online coaching clients I had:

For blessing me with the opportunity to better their lives.

My ex-fiancées:

The women I was engaged to. The ladies I considered my best friends for our respective relationships. You provided great inspiration for my next romantic adventure.

Anyone mentioned by name (whether I know them personally or not):

For your influence.

Welcome

Hello, you beautiful Huns, Kins, and Loves!!

How are you?

In *The Midst of CHAOS: Manifesting Life Through Co-Creation*? When I think of that, I can think of different points in my life. My journey is multi-dimensional. It always has been. It always will be (to be honest).

My name is Zachary Shiloh Watts. I am a multiple-time bestselling author. I am the Holistic Health Coach behind what I call Mind Over Matter Unlimited. I am the host of the *BLK Lion's Airspace* podcast. BLK is short for black.

I've been a writer for years. Writing was, is, and will be a saving grace. It motivates me to do right. Paved the way for me to correct my share of wrongdoing. I am eternally blessed to have this ability.

I originally wrote this book (you are reading) in early spring 2022. I got rid of what I wrote. Why? I had a different extension than Manifesting Life Through Co-Creation. I wasn't feeling like I wanted to write my solo book. I was focused on wrapping up getting whatever co-authorings I yearned for.

As I thought about things on June 3, 2022, I was in CHAOS. My co-authoring scheduling went through some rough changes. I had a clear path. My noble plan went to Hell.

I can hear you... *"Well, dude. How did that happen?"*

We'll get there. This is an adventure. One I never really forgot. Full of "Coming to Jesus" moments. Full of failures. What makes me a general human being.

To get to where I am now, we're going to start from the beginning. Let's see me as I weathered my share of storms. It's been over 3 years since this book really manifested.

Fall 2019 & Journal Writing

It is November 3, 2019.

I am an overweight Type II diabetic (who had nasty anxiety and depression). I asked my doctor to send me to a therapist. I was unknowingly losing my fiancée. I didn't want to bother other people about her, our problems, etc.

Several hours have passed since a Catholic church service. My surrogate dad went to eat with his sister (and her hubby). I was awaiting dinner from my woman. She was journaling in her room. I noticed what she was doing.

There was still time to go out. I decided to go to my local CVS. I had some ExtraCare bucks. I wanted to start journaling. I did my research into it.

I still laugh at myself that I forgot my store currency. That was fine. I will always remember that I got my supplies for $15.66. I left the store happy with stuff to aid me in the weight loss journey.

I returned to where I was living. I had my dinner. Wrote in my journal once I said good night to my hun. I recounted the whole day (best as I could). When I was done, I felt some sense of pride.

Weight by body wasn't the only thing knocking me down. Same with gradually losing the best friend I ever had. I felt disrespected by my employer (which was a nursing home located here in Staten Island, New York). I wanted to not only write about my general thoughts.

I would return to CVS within 5 days. I purchased two more journals. The first was to record my journey to gain new employment. The other was to help me with my food and medications.

I would take my journals with me where I could. Different places such as St. Joseph's church, my work home, and the Staten Island Mall. I would just write about what I ate, general thoughts, and hopes to manifest.

People were starting to notice me. They were telling me about myself. They saw I didn't fit in my clothes (quite so much). I was more attentive. More friendly than I used to be.

I didn't really notice myself being too heavy. I knew something had changed. I was more carefree. I did let go, release, accept, or whatever you would like to say.

I stopped my bitching about being paid minimum wage (by the 2018 New York State mandate). I did leave the woman I loved (on November 23, 2019). I had no social media in my face daily (since October 28 & 29, 2019). I saw nothing (or anyone) but myself.

Before I knew it, time had really flown by. People wanted to know about what I had done. How I had lost so much weight. Even my new doctor was awed by me.

BLK Lion's Roar (Solo Version)

The original BLK Lion's Roar?

I began this whole writing-a-book saga with that. I got asses to talk about how much I changed. A blonde woman saw me as *"her hero."* Suggested that I write a book.

"You lost so much weight in the last several months. The world should know about it. You got me to try my best".

I would ask people if they were interested. I wasn't gonna put my energy towards something if there was no heat for such. There seemed to be more than one person agreeing. I said, *"Okay, why not?".*

The title of BLK Lion's Roar. How did that come? It was kinda simple. I took BLK Lion (which is part of my podcast's name). I had to speak. Another word for speak (for me) is roar.

I began writing it on March 31, 2020. It would be quite a journey. I mainly used my journals for it. I wrote the sucka for several months. I seldom added freestyle points.

I would go some days doing it. There would be times when nothing was coming. Fear started to seep in. It would lead to me going for nearly four months.

I was getting desperate. BLK Lion's Roar was becoming a chore. I wanted help. I wound up paying for shipping to a book that I never fully finished reading. The book was called *"Write a Saleable Book in 10-Minute Bursts of Madness"* by Nicholas Boothman.

Zachary Shiloh Blacks Out

The pressure of writing a book ultimately won. I set BLK Lion's Roar aside. I believe the overwhelm got me in the summer of 2020.

I blacked out (or fainted), waiting for a bus. What happened to me is unknown. I know I did eat that morning. What I recall was living part of a lyric to a song called *"Wide Awake"* by Katy Perry.

I woke up right on the concrete. I dinged my head under a metal mailbox. I was blessed to make it to St. Joseph's Church on time. I wanted to support my surrogate dad (who had a service for his dearly departed wife).

I made it to his house (post-service). Stayed some hours. Got back to my parents' house. I wound up learning more about what happened to me.

I wasn't having electrolytes in my body. I wasn't a heavy salt user. I mainly ran on fruit. I had to start incorporating stuff that my body needed.

Here I am (two-plus years later), saying I am happy and grateful it did happen. This was a significant learning experience.

Universal Laws

After I left my second fiancée, I was browsing around YouTube. I wanted my soulmate. The quote-unquote one. I found several videos.

According to the people I watched, they all obtained what I sought. Not only did they manifest their (version of what Zachary Shiloh calls) Honeykins. They made lives that dreams are made of. Each person I saw had attributed their success to a Universal Law called the Law of Attraction.

That same intention brought me numerous people. My very first successful self-help teacher was named Michele Elder. She is better known as Michele Joy. Michele Joy was the hostess of a podcast called *Law of Attraction in Action*.

I found her podcast by way of Anchor.fm. Anchor was where I recorded my BLK Lion's Airspace podcast (before it became Spotify for Podcasters). At the point where I found Michele, I was about six months into my podcasting career. She was holding her beginning of 2020 Zoom call (precisely on New Year's Day). I didn't hesitate to be part of it.

I made the right decision. Every minute was well spent. I had a purpose. I left with a word for the year. My word was determination. That was exactly what I had.

My next teacher was named Katherine Hurst. She had a bit more pull than Michele. That's no disrespect to the Portland,

Oregon, mother of two. What do I mean by more pull? Katherine had stronger ties in the self-help world.

This would bring me more teachers. This would aid me as the world was entering a new era. Some say we never truly recovered from it. That is known as The Coronavirus Pandemic.

In the mind of Zachary Shiloh Watts, he didn't know the difference between epidemic and pandemic. All I knew was suffering. All I felt was universal agony. Businesses were shut down for weeks or permanently. The human race was forced to be masked in public while adhering to being socially distanced six feet apart.

What I sought (in bringing me a female companion) gave me not just teachers. It opened me up to worlds bigger than I saw. I unknowingly would go on to clear years of generational fears. I would find that forgiveness wasn't just for others, but it was to give for myself.

One of the most significant quotes said, *"He who forgets the past is surely to repeat it."* I never forgot the past completely. I didn't just for the sake of photographic memory. Every single self-help teacher I would have (after Katherine Hurst and Michele Joy) wouldn't let me forget common themes.

We are all energetic beings living a human experience. Like does attract like. Our thoughts can manifest in physical form. Where space goes, energy does grow.

She Is Magic & DreamBuilder

Earlier in this book, I mentioned the original BLK Lion's Roar and how I did the best I could to make my baby into a solo book. You saw the result. It went nowhere, really (on that front).

Months into my working with the Universal Laws, I was paralleling with a growing book series. That series is called *She Is Magic*. The first book was released on March 31, 2020 (according to Amazon.com). What is March 31, 2020? It was the exact date that BLK Lion's Roar was being manifested.

I didn't know of the *She Is Magic* series immediately. I wasn't only working on BLK Lion's Roar. I believe I graduated from the *"Law of Attraction"* course by Katherine Hurst. I was finished with a different one called *"Unsinkable"* by Sonia Ricotti.

I was registered in a "new" self-help/Law of Attraction course called *"DreamBuilder."* It was made by Mary Morrissey. Like with Katherine Hurst, I would work with Mary Morrissey for 90 days. What I did was reinforce what I mentioned.

When I was done with the actual *DreamBuilder* course, I returned to social media (a few weeks prior). I could feel a tug to go to the *DreamBuilder* community. It was by the Brave Thinking Institute. Brave Thinking Institute is the company that Mary Morrissey (and her three children) runs.

I was answering random posts. I even made a post (or more) myself there too. I could feel a sense of belonging. My interactions would tie into something I was unaware of.

A woman (by the name of Linda Carducci) messaged me (in June 2020). Linda would go on to become my spiritual mother. We would make our own *DreamBuilder* community. It would be the both of us with some mutual friends (or acquaintances).

Linda pulled me aside for a one-on-one chat. We went over how our week was, what we did in *DreamBuilder*, and whatever else. She loved how passionate I was about my podcast. She noticed my passion for writing was stronger.

What Linda recommended awed me. I had no clue how it would affect me multi-dimensional. Linda had ties to the writing industry. She suggested that I talk to a friend of hers.

I believe one of two things happened. The first was Linda sent me the Facebook page of said person. The other was I looked into this individual (through Linda's friends list). That human being was Blair Hayse.

There was something about Blair. I really gravitated towards her. It wasn't just a sexual attraction (from me to her). I felt her magical energy. When I combed through her Facebook page, I found more than what Linda described.

Remember me mentioning that I had a blackout in 2020? What if I told you I never forgot that incident for a positive reason? The same evening, Blair Hayse and I became friends on Facebook.

I approached Blair to join me in my BLK Lion's Domain interview segment. I did my best to see if she did any other interviews. I found an interview. Blair would explain to me that she rarely did podcasts. I wasn't completely shocked.

I was happy and grateful to Blair. I expressed that to her. We kept in touch as we transitioned from summer to the start of fall 2020. We supported each other in Facebook posts.

September 20, 2020, is a date I don't want to ever forget. It was when Blair made what would be unknowingly the first of multiple appearances on my show. I did something for her that I did for no other woman prior. The Mississippi Magical Miracles Woman had me in a blazer.

We would record our episode in less than an hour. Blair got to hype her forthcoming Step into Your Magic virtual summit (which began the following day). I made her laugh. We gelled pretty well off each other. Please use the following link to listen:

https://anchor.fm/blklionsairspace/episodes/BLK-Lions-Airspace-Episode-184---Roaming-Around-With-Blair-Hayse-ek27d0

They Are Magic

Blair's appearance not only gave me what would become one of my greatest podcast recordings. I featured some people who I knew. Some people I interviewed were already influencers throughout the years (especially in the general podcasting world).

Blair did something I believe no one did. She became my mentor right on the air. She wanted to help bring out my potential as a writer. How? I'm still floored years later.

Blair was looking for writers to be in her first book of 2021 called *They Are Magic*. We chatted about the aforementioned BLK Lion's Roar. How I wrote my story, then BLR collected cobwebs for months. I was offered my slot in *They Are Magic* (as we wrapped up Blair's episode).

I have this recurring thing after it happened. I even mentioned it to Blair herself (when she shockingly returned to my podcast nearly a year later). I thought Blair was pulling my leg. She didn't jive me on my show.

So, five days did eventually pass (like true time does). I thought about Blair. I did keep the on-air promise I made to the self-made CEO. I bought her Step into Your Magic fall summit. I watched all that I could (before my purchase).

I really wanted BLK Lion's Roar to be published. I didn't know when another opportunity to do so (would arrive or come to me). Why not go with someone who has been a proven success? Why not put my hands in that of a woman who had her own business (before she was 40 years old)?

So, I signed up for *They Are Magic* on September 25, 2020. September 25th had a place in my heart. Two years prior, I had joined the *Let's Voltron* podcast (for a Voltron Legendary Defender two-episode review). That was my first real-time speaking on any media platform. It would be the catalyst to get BLK Lion's Airspace roaring.

When I signed on for *They Are Magic*, my work home (of five plus years) still paid me (following my August 28th termination for Coronavirus budget reasoning). I had started a new job that I unknowingly would leave (in less than a month). I charged my card. I began paying for my slot. It would take me several months to finish, but I was happy to be in the book.

I made double history with my payment. According to Blair herself, I was the very first person to be in *They Are Magic*. I was the very first male to be in her overall Magic series. I didn't take these for granted. I am still humbled over two years later.

The general process was genuinely being in school with an elite group of people. I would learn the dos and don'ts of being a published author. I reduced BLK Lion's Roar from seventeen pages down to five.

Being in *They Are Magic* didn't just help me get my story published. I was invited to this big three-day event by Blair's coach, Crystal Anne Davis. She was no thrills. She didn't bullshit you.

At that point, I had been with my present job about two months. I was blessed that Crystal wanted to work with me. I left 2020 with her as my mentor. Linda and Blair credited her each for their successes. Why can I not do the same?

I got to work with Crystal every week in January 2021. She went over stuff that made her successful. I loved how uncensored she was. She was her authentic self. I expected nothing but the absolute best from my coach.

I had an accountability partner named Jayme. We met for a few Zoom calls. Did an episode of my podcast. Stayed in touch for the remainder of *High Digital Income Nomad* (Crystal's program I was taking).

Time moves forward with more excitement. I got to interview some of my co-authors from *They Are Magic* (before we got to the book release date). Speaking of BLK Lion's Airspace, I was going through a pivot (as Blair would say) with BLK Lion's Domain. I was noticing people I surrounded myself with.

My co-workers weren't staying where we were supposed to be. It bothered me to some degree (at the time). This made me think that BLK Lion's Domain had to change. I'm technically not Roaming Around. When I have a guest, we're sitting on our tushies.

I was expecting Stephanie Mahony to join me in BLK Lion's Domain. Roaming Around in BLK Lion's Domain was dead. I needed something different. I could hear Linda Carducci (in my head). She always used to say that I needed to be grounded.

I was walking to the bus stop (as I was reflecting). I didn't want BLK Lion's Domain to be gone. That was the name of my interview segment (regardless of the extended name). I kept hearing grounding. I heard *"being grounded by the universe."*

Being grounded by the universe? BLK Lion's Domain? Universal Grounding in BLK Lion's Domain. It suited me better than Roaming Around ever did. Makes more sense as I retell this story more uncensored.

I was attracting Reiki masters. I was becoming friends with people who did meditation. I was associating myself with helping others to unlock their supernatural abilities.

All of this occurs just as my thirty-third year of life wraps up. I became thirty-four within mere weeks of BLK Lion's Domain's next extension being born. As January transitioned to February, there was one very powerful moment. I didn't remember the actual date for a long time.

I remembered that *They Are Magic* was being promoted. I did so on my podcast. I made posts on Facebook more than Twitter and Instagram.

Blair Hayse called all of us authors into the Facebook group. I can confirm that it was February 10, 2021. How? I did a search on July 17, 2022 (after revamping this book again).

Laughs a bit.

Blair asked, *"Who is the opening chapter in They Are Magic?"* Tammy Lambrou (my beloved Tammy Love, as I called her) responded, *"Zachary Shiloh."* I just got in from work, read the post, and replied *"Oh, Blairkins. Is it a certain roar?"*

What came out of Blair Hayse shocked me. She revealed that we had a male opener. It wasn't me. It was the only other non-Caucasian guy.

Blair did address me. She said that BLK Lion's Roar was the FINAL chapter. I didn't know how to react. I believe that night I got on my knees. I may have cried myself to sleep positively.

I believe I was in the same boat as Tammy. I thought BLK Lion's Roar would be the opening chapter to *They Are Magic*. When I look at things, Blair made the right decision. Why? We had a male to open.

Why not me? Not to toot my own horn, but I was the first male in her overall book series. Blair must have believed (in her heart) that I was worthy of ending the first unisex book (beyond that). When she reads this, I say *"Thank you"* to Blairkins again.

I announced my *They Are Magic* position in two forms. I took to my Airspace to vocalize it after Blair made a post (regarding how she felt as we entered launch week). I did another from Facebook in the early hours of February 11th (just as I was preparing for work).

I felt more bonded to my mentor. Here was this woman who had numerous book launches. A multiple-timed bestselling author stated (for the world) that she was scared. She was nervous about *They Are Magic*.

This caused me to remember *The Fast and The Furious* (by one of my general fave directors named Rob Cohen). I loved the racing stuff (like any fan of those films). I loved the heart-to-heart shit even more. Why?

The talks were where you got to know the character. You get to understand the person's motives. Why they are who they are. What happened to them.

My favorite character is Dominic Toretto. Dom was the King of the L.A. racing world. The leader of this group they called The Team. More so, he is known for his love of family.

He explains that he was scared to drive this 1970 Dodge Charger (that he and his father worked on). He left it alone, especially after his father died (in an accident). Dom would eventually overcome his fear. From that point forward, he was seen in some form of Dodge Charger (in every *Fast and Furious* film) he was in (minus *Tokyo Drift*).

They Are Magic was my Dodge Charger. I was scared shitless of it. I didn't know what my future held. I was blessed to be a published author.

February 16, 2021, was the day that *They Are Magic* was released. I woke up before 5 AM EST. I had a copy of the book as author magic. I spent several hours reading. Every story was very moving.

There was a Zoom call. I wasn't missing it. As I sit wrapping up my thoughts on this nearly year-long writing culmination, I remember almost everyone involved. I believe both editors were available. Blair wasn't all dolled up (as she was known to be).

I recall being the only male involved. The eldest guy wasn't available because of his time zone and the opening chapter writer was occupied with only God knows. I was happy and grateful to be on.

We went over the day ahead. We went crazy about the fact that our book was released. All of the Huns involved laugh their asses off at me, saying, *"I'm in The Flow State."* I made it known that I read every chapter.

The call wasn't long. It lasted for thirty minutes. Off to the races up until 5 PM EST. I did my best to post every half hour. I didn't care if I got lost in the shuffle.

I was there to support not just myself. I was there for Blairkins. I was there for Jayme. I was there for everyone else who wrote a chapter.

We weren't alone. Previous *She Is Magic* book writers were with us. They were doing posts on our behalf. If not, then just reacting to our stuff. Keeping our family going as seconds eventually became hours.

Beginning My Survival in a Retail Jungle

This company has been in my life since 2014. I was a Continuing Education student at Kingsborough Community College. I needed textbooks for my Medical Billing and Coding course. I got what I required for a better price than what my school charged. I would go on to become a faithful customer for several years.

I had no clue what making a single account would do. I didn't envision how it would change my life. There was no idea of me being associated with a work environment. I didn't foresee the unlocking of my true self.

All I wanted was to be a Medical Office Assistant. I would do two runs with the Kingsborough Continuing Ed. My first was done on Saturday mornings from late 2013 through Summer 2014. The second was on Wednesday evenings during the Summer of 2015. Both would result in me transitioning from volunteer to paid employment in 2016.

I mentioned what happened to me. Before my unforeseen departure in 2020, I shared with people some details from my Fall 2019 Journal Writing about how I felt disrespected by my employer and how I worked for minimum wage since December 2018.

My frustrations began before the 2018 New York City mandating. I was being paid the same pay for over two years.

I felt like I was in Intermediate School through college again. What do I mean? I wasn't just working as a Business Office Clerk.

I was working for Medical Supplies. I went to college for office work. I did the work required in the retail industry. I was feeling as if I returned to college for nothing.

People told me to look for work elsewhere. One place opened up just as my frustrations were being born. The consensus of loved ones suggested I go there. When I heard this, I was laughing my ass off. I thought it was a bloody joke.

Fast forward a month (and some days) after being terminated. I had signed up for *They Are Magic*. I was gaining a stronger awareness (of my newly acquired job). I wasn't for having to be outside (to get carts together) as the seasons changed. I wound up talking to someone I haven't chatted with (in a long time).

As this unexpected discussion ended, I wound up being employed in the referred jungle. My exact hire date was October 11, 2020. My new hire screening was within three days. I first touched the retail terrain several days later.

It is said that the first week to a month of something is the hardest. Whoever said that was telling the truth (if you believe it to be such). Zachary Shiloh Watts felt that fully in his heart, mind, body, and soul. It really hit me sometime after my orientation.

I learned this thing called Palletizing. I couldn't stand it. I was scanning packages with a scan gun. I did this from 7:15 AM to 5:45 PM. My scheduled days were Wednesday, Thursday, Friday, and Saturday.

I did that for an exact month. The exact day I decreed being done with Palletizing would unknowingly pivot my career. I would find a more down-to-earth division.

I took Sunday, Monday, and Tuesday to rest. I was charged for the following Wednesday. I didn't bother going to get a scan gun. I just headed to what would make me "famous."

When I started, it was more "Trial by Fire" than consistent. Only a selected few were honored with staying. I was curious as to why this was. I questioned people I got to know.

Folks didn't like their experience. They felt this guy I called "Captain Blood" was an insensitive asshole. The work was more vigorous hell on their bodies (than what I stopped doing daily).

I wasn't going to be deterred. I was determined to learn my craft. I picked up on things quickly.

I was surrounded by these yellow bins called totes. They housed items to be packed, picked, or shipped out (by other divisions). They were empty, where I yearned to be. There were four machines that produced them. Each completed version was 11 pieces high.

When the machines were wonky, a person (or two) had to downstack. Once there was a reasonable amount of completed totes, co-workers would put them on blue mats. A genuinely full product had a top (or cover, as someone would say). The finished item is placed on a truck and then shipped out.

Wolverine vs Sabretooth (Becoming A Leader then Manifesting My Greatest Workplace Foe)

As I continued being under Captain Blood, I noticed a difference in scheduling. He and the main crew worked Sunday through Wednesday. Thursday through Saturday had no "Leader." I worked with the insensitive asshole once a week.

I originally came to work early to sharpen my skills. Not only that, but I knew I was definitely on time. I took it further. I clocked in an hour early each day I worked.

One day, my career changed. Someone asked me, *"Who is in charge?"* I felt a tug in my heart. I took up the mantle of Tote Stacker Leader (from Thursday through Saturday). I replied, *"I am."* As the saying goes, it was off to the races for me.

I did my absolute best to teach new people the system. This inspired me to improve myself (as a general worker). I would listen to suggestions and then implement what suited me. I believe this began getting me positive reactions. Before I knew it, time was flying by quicker than ever.

It was February 2021. I have been the Leader of Tote Stacker for a quarter of a year. My team and I were doing our best. By building on what I learned, I was gaining momentum as the Leader. Some people kinda even hailed me as a "Hero."

There would end up being a shift (or pivot, as Blair Hayse would say) that occurred. I drew the attention of an authority figure. We went on to have a private chat (where he told me that I wasn't the Tote Stacker Leader). The man claimed he wanted to "center" Tote Stacker around me (with a team of consistent people).

I already had specific people in mind. Some had worked with Captain Blood. Others were purely with me. I believed in their work ethic. If they were away, they'd return to me (whenever they were ready to do so).

I told Sabretooth (as I would call him) to give me my specific people. These were the best workers to me. I didn't get what I wanted. That didn't sit well with me. Not one single bit of it.

There were times when extra hands were needed. My right-hand man (whom I called Angelito) would tell management. We received personnel to aid us. Sabretooth would rear his Bill Cosby-looking self and then take away folks. This became a recurring theme.

Remember how I said I would clock in early? I arrived at work one day. Sabretooth tells me the company policy for clocking in. Thank you for the notification, but the actions following got me heated.

As I wrapped up my talk with him, Sabretooth had me do two things. I clocked out of the time I was working. I had to wait until 7:15 AM exactly. This made me feel like my work was worthless. It really did.

Sabretooth would draw more of my Wolverine side. He took me away from Tote Stacker at times. The man talked shit behind my back to others. This idiot dissed me (while in my presence). All of his sins were adding to my ire.

He got me to a level that no person ever did. I was willing to violate a specific company policy purposefully. There were instances where people had to calm me down. In different moments, I literally had to be held back. Sabretooth got me wanting to cause bodily harm.

The issues between us culminated into a six-month saga. A miracle happened in the summer of 2021. Our story would come to an end. Why? Sabretooth got moved to nighttime. I know I wasn't the only happy person.

When I heard that news, it was like a block party.

People were practically dancing.

I am completely serious.

Letters of Magic

The road to this book really began as the world entered 2021. I have been with Blair Hayse for several months. I was a fresh new online coach for nearly a month. BLK Lion's Domain was a month plus away from one full year.

Speaking of BLK Lion's Domain, I was looking for guests. I remember talking to Blair about it. She was okay with me using her now Elite Author Group. I made a post. Blair herself vouched for me (by letting the others know that she had fun while promoting stuff).

Several women actually said yes to me. One, as I said earlier, was Stephanie Mahony. Another was Jayme. The most memorable was Jennifer Kirch.

Jennifer stood out in different ways. She was one half of Blair's editing team. I found out when I got BLK Lion's Roar back to do my second round of edits. I believe Jennifer messaged me in private.

I was in awe. I thought that Amanda Goddard (or Amanda Please, as I'd go on to call her) was gonna edit BLK Lion's Roar the whole three times. No disrespect to Amanda, but there was something a little more soulful about Jennifer.

I'm not saying that Amanda isn't a sweetheart in her own right. She is damn good at what she does. That's why she became the Senior Editor of Elite Publishing House. Let's get back to Jennifer.

Jennifer was very inspirational. She was the main reason I stayed with Blair Hayse Publishing (outside of Blairkins herself). I wanted to work with her. I was praying that Blair would continue being unisex. I hoped Jenn would eventually be part of the same book as a co-author.

They Are Magic is wrapping up. We get to February. We are a mere eleven days from the launch date. Blair announced to her Alumni group that she was getting out of her comfort zone.

She had a new book she wanted to do. It is a book on letters. The people involved were to write to someone. I was up for returning.

I was talking to Blairkins about *Letters of Magic* (in private). She was hyped for it. She was hoping that I was returning. I believe I asked for a payment plan. I began paying right there.

It is the launch day for *They Are Magic*. The book is a hit in multiple categories on Amazon. It has lived the name across the world. We, the present writers, are celebrating with alumni.

Blair reminds us that *Letters of Magic* goes on public sale the next day. My silly ass thought that Blair was gonna start work on the doggone thing then. I was happily wrong. She pulled her Magic family in for a nice huddle.

Jenn Kirch was in that exact chat. She mentioned that she was returning to the Magic series. She wasn't doing the forward. She gave me my wish to be co-authors together.

I believe Jenn and I did talk privately. We were excited to be in the same book. I respectfully asked if she was okay to do our BLK Lion's Domain after *They Are Magic* was released. Jenn said she was good with that.

March 15, 2021, was a date I never forgot. It was a day before *They Are Magic* was a month old (post-release). I was having a shitacular day at work. I was in the process of merging my coaching, podcasting, and writing into one brand. I couldn't find a name.

As my shift was ending, I heard the word *"Flowtastic."* Flowtastic (or my version of it) was what I used for a defunct podcast called *"Doing Business in The Flow." Doing Business in The Flow* was hosted by Linda Carducci. It was recorded by me. We didn't go anywhere with it due to conflicting schedules.

I wrapped up work for the day. I zoomed on home. I wanted to tell Linda about my business name. I got on Facebook, and then what followed shook me to my core.

Blair announced that Jennifer Kirch had died. She lost her battle against cancer. No disrespect to the Almighty Blairkins, but she was wrong. Jenn didn't lose. Our friend was a winner.

Some people never lived to be Jenn's age. I was happy and grateful to her. She was a successful person. She did her best with time on Earth. We should be celebrating whatever time we had with this angel.

My podcast was paid (at the time). I did my best to do an actual tribute for Jenn. I didn't have a script (like I usually do on recordings). I wasn't paid at all. The money didn't matter.

I had one thing on my mind. That was the love I had for her. Trying to convey what she meant to me. How much she influenced Blair, myself, and other Magic family members.

Speaking of my podcast, it went on to be unpaid in spring 2021. I only had my day-to-day job. It sucked for me to only have something I didn't really like as my primary income source. That wasn't my only problem.

My Love's Roar coaching was going nowhere. I lost one client. I gained another, and then schedule conflicts made me release her. I would spend seasons floundering with it.

Some people would cuss my ass out for what I am about to say. I am happy and grateful for Jenn Kirch's passing. Why? I eventually found out who to write my Letter of Magic to.

I was struggling to find someone to write about. Everyone knew how much I loved Blairkins. Couldn't go with Jayme for reasons I shall not express. Unbeknownst to me, I was losing other people I thought I would be friends with forever.

I was redoing a course I was in. It is based on *May Cause Miracles* (by Gabrielle Bernstein). The program was made by a gay couple (who were legit friends of Gabby). They were my coaches for several months.

I believe Blair was finally on maternity leave. She was preparing for the birth of her youngest child. She was gonna be scarcely available to talk (more than she usually is). I got a hold of her one day.

My Letter of Magic was manifested from *May Cause Miracles*. I did submit what I had to Blair. I was unaware of the word limit, but I wound up sending it to Amanda Please. When I heard that I had to write more, I wasn't completely happy.

This bothered me for a day (or two). I had a mutual friend with Blair (who never wrote alongside us). She did Facebook live readings (twice a week). She had a better connection to source energy, God, or _____. I was so flushed that I paid for my reading.

I got my answer. I was told that I'll get my Letter of Magic done. I went to bed that night with some relief. From that point onward, it was Flowtastic.

The title couldn't just be BLK Lion's Roar II. I'm a writer. I'm a storyteller. There had to be an extension. Something to hook readers.

Okay. Paying homage to a friend? She was an angel to many. She helped me find a way to unify my coaching, podcasting, and writing. Tribute to a Flowtastic Angel.

BLK Lion's Roar II: Tribute to a Flowtastic Angel was my Letter of Magic. It fit Jenn Kirch perfectly. I wasn't where I was without her. It was an excellent name for such an inspirational human being.

What I had did called for more. There is no doubt in my mind. I had something nice; however, something was missing. I was telling people about Blairkins' relationship with Jenn than my own.

I remembered all I mentioned earlier. Jenn's general influence. Having BLK Lion's Roar edited by her. Accepting an interview with me. Having *They Are Magic* foreword written by Jenn.

Every time my letter was due, I was first to hand my work in. The edits went through like clockwork. Amanda Please had worked her magic. Amanda was so good (that I told Blair) that I recommended her to be in charge of Blair Hayse Publishing (during the owner's remaining leave).

The actual co-authors were incredible to be with. Tammy Love returned from *They Are Magic*. This pixy hun named Geneva Hill represented *She Is Magic, Too*. My homie (from Texas) named Brooke was back from *She Is Magic, Yes*.

With every Magic series book, there were new additions to the family. Charlie Scanlon was the only other guy. Sarrah Papa Smith blessed us from Canada.

Being worried is part of human nature. So is having anger. Crying so hard that one falls asleep. To say I didn't go through these is bogus.

Jenn Kirch's death was a massive blow for the general Magic series family. She wasn't just an editor of BLK Lion's Roar. She wasn't only a multiple-time best-selling author. She was our hype woman.

Everyone I knew missed her. No one missed her more than Blair. We would add another blow to the family. Sometime after her birth, Blair's youngest daughter would stay in the hospital longer than we expected.

We all were concerned for the newborn. Her mother wasn't just a literary figure. It was hard (especially for me) to watch as my greatest influence could lose her child. *Letters of Magic* was delayed. Part of me thought that it would not see the light of day.

I kept love in my heart alive. Believing that the baby is her mother in a younger form. River Rose would feed on our energy. Blair herself would have peace. The general Hayse family would get to be with the kid.

Prayer does work. It's not just something religious. It isn't only "Please help _____". It's energy channeling. It's a focus for positive outcomes.

River Rose isn't alive for the sake of Blair. Not only to get *Letters of Magic* back on course. I believe Jenn Kirch was needed on the other side to help all of us. Knowing that makes me say more that we honored the Flowtastic Angel multiple times.

Once the water flower child got out of the hospital, there was no stopping *Letters of Magic*. Blair was conducting Facebook Lives. We got our promotional pictures. The book was promoted daily.

The release date was August 3, 2021. The date was already for me. Zachary Shiloh Watts became an older brother in 1989. Just like the Hayse family, our youngest was a girl.

I got an intuitive hit as we got closer. Blair did the final hype video twenty-four hours prior. Blair made the announcement. I said, *"Oh shit."*

As I did with *They Are Magic*, I made time to read. The order was magical. I almost know everyone's story by heart. At the time, I was more moved than with *They Are Magic*.

I wasn't the final chapter again. My position rocked my world. Who was the end to *Letters of Magic?* Brooke. I was the chapter right before her.

I got on the Zoom call. I was the first person on. I don't go crazy with using my race much, but seeing myself and Purr Hun (Brooke) together made me proud to be black. I made it known to Blairkins. I thanked her.

Speaking of being black, I'd like to talk about it briefly. I am the middle child of an all-black family. I wasn't raised where blacks had "no rights." I didn't grow up having to fight to use the bathroom with Caucasians.

I wasn't like my mother, who was frantic (when I ran out of a video store) and then told me not to do it (because of my ethnicity). I wasn't like my father, who (was heavy in politics then) tried to weaponize people (who looked like us) to get me to vote. I never saw myself only as a black man. The likes of Malcolm X, Martin Luther King, and Rosa Parks died to bring humanity together.

Being in *They Are Magic* and *Letters of Magic* (in my respective positions) wasn't because of my skin tone. I earned them by who I am. I was there by co-existing with others (regardless of their origins). I was a human being. I do what I do in honor of all nationalities.

All nationalities involved in *They Are Magic* worked as one. We posted on all forms of social media until we hit the top spot. I joined a rare breed of writers on that day.

Ascension Visionary Leaders

It is March 6, 2021. We are ten days away from *They Are Magic* being a month old. I am getting ready to transition from one work schedule to another.

My last working Saturday is total Hell. My team, for the most part, left work early. My division looks like Armageddon hits.

A certain Sabretooth is threatening me. I have two options. I help him, or I leave. Well, you don't disrespect me, then think I'll stay. I left right after lunch.

I head straight home. I made my dinner. I ate my apples with oats. Later I had tangerines with scrap pork meat.

I cuddle in my bed. I noticed I started reading a certain book. Let's cheer me up (from the shitstorm of my final Wednesday through Saturday).

Ascension is the book's name. It's compiled by Janet Brent. The same woman who was in the original *She Is Magic*.

She is not alone. There is a Surfer Hun. We have an Indigenous. A Dragon is flying. A Rose blessing this union. Last is a plus-sized introverted male.

I dedicated some hours to my reading. Every minute kept me going. Each author touched my soul somehow. I was clapping my hands by the end.

I was so excited that I made a Facebook post. Thanked each person for their contributions. DMs (or private messages) were sent by me. Not only was gratitude shown, but all were invited to be guests on my podcast.

Please use the provided links.

Dion Garcia:

BLK Lion's Airspace Episode 357 - Universal Grounding in BLK Lion's Domain with Dion Garcia by BLK Lion's Airspace (anchor.fm)

Caryn Terres:

BLK Lion's Airspace Episode 366 - Universal Grounding in BLK Lion's Domain with Caryn Terres by BLK Lion's Airspace (anchor.fm)

Janet Brent:

BLK Lion's Airspace Episode 388 - Universal Grounding in BLK Lion's Domain with Janet Brent by BLK Lion's Airspace (anchor.fm)

Alecia Rose:

BLK Lion's Airspace Episode 391 - Universal Grounding in BLK Lion's Domain with Alecia Rose by BLK Lion's Airspace (anchor.fm)

I did not know if (or when) Blair Hayse would do another unisex Magic book. I was talking to Janet almost every day (about wanting to be in this series). Time flew by. I knew I had some financial issues, but I believed in myself. I knew I could make some payments.

June 5, 2021, is when I joined Ascension Visionary Leaders. My story was called *BLK Lion's Roar III: My Flowtastic Adventure Part I*. It was my tale, from watching Berry Gordy's *The Last Dragon* to my reveal as a supernatural being (on my podcast).

Ascension Visionary Leaders was a rather unique work experience. I was with Blair Hayse Publishing twice. I was used to the edits from two editors in *They Are Magic*. One only from March onward. I had three rounds.

When I left Blairkins, I had no clue who does edits for Janet Brent. I recalled being messaged by Jan. We were talking about My Flowtastic Adventure. As the conversation kept rocking along, I had an *"Excuse me, mam"* moment.

Jan was already badass. I knew of her talents when I signed on. One was her helping design covers for the *She Is Magic* books. With *Ascension*, I learned that a publisher could do the editing. Magic Hun was our editor.

We worked on Flowtastic Adventure together. I had fun, however long it took. I had a newfound respect when it was done. I believe I even said that to her.

The first week of August 2021 wasn't only when *Letters of Magic* was released. Two more beautiful gifts were bestowed upon me. I spoke of having teachers in the Universal Laws chapter. A reminder that the biggest known in pop culture is the Law of Attraction.

I mentioned earlier that I was in Mary Morrissey's *DreamBuilder* program. There was a more live version of it called *Brave Thinking Masters*. Mary would teach on Thursday nights. I was making payments on it until August 17, 2020.

As I said, I transitioned from a nursing home to two other places in less than two months. I wouldn't pay anything again until some days before Thanksgiving. The final 2020 payment was eleven days prior to Christmas.

I became so busy that I forgot I owed money to Mary Morrissey. I tried to make payments again in small bursts starting in June 2021. Something was better than nothing, right?

I received a phone call from the *Brave Thinking Institute*. I explained my situation to the representative. I basically said this: *"I'm willing to do whatever I can to pay this grand sum."* I was ready to make a payment on August 5, 2021.

As I went to pay, I saw something that I never forgot. I was $7,600 in debt. It was entirely gone. I checked myself at different times. I am still humble and grateful for it a year or so later.

We get to the launch of *Ascension Visionary Leaders*. I continued my tradition of reading on the actual launch day. History was made on multiple fronts.

BLK Lion's Roar III: My Flowtastic Adventure was the opening chapter. I, Zachary Shiloh, was the only guy in that book. I was one of three non-Caucasians. The non-Caucasians were the majority of writers. One of these three happened to be our Asian publisher.

There was something I didn't know that was happening. Supposedly, there is a supernatural phenomenon that occurs every year in August. It is called the Lion's Gate. It perks strong on August 8th.

As you read, I have numerous things under BLK Lion. I felt the Lion's Gate energy that exact day. It anointed not just me, but the entire writing cast of Ascension Visionary Leaders.

There was no Blair Hayse Zoom call this go. No jonesing out how good the book was to the writers in a private meeting. There was no setup to make the day magical. I was straight to promoting the book (ala social media posts) all day I could.

I didn't even really talk to Jan Brent that day. She was handling not just our book. Magic Hun was making magic in numerous ways.

Two to three of the five writers were promoting the book all day. One was Molly Murray. Moll Doll had her own Lion's Gate celebration to host. I was happy and grateful that she helped for a bit. Speaking of Moll Doll, she did eventually get interviewed by me.

Please listen here:

https://spotifyanchor-web.app.link/e/nMq9mpHM1yb

The day ends with me realizing something I did twice. I did it for the first time without the Almighty Blairkins. It would be the setup for quite a bigger journey.

Huns, Kins, and Loves

At this point in the book, you may have burning questions. Why are you calling people Hun, Kins, and Love? What's the deal with these nicknames? Can you explain this?

I said this in an episode of my podcast. I was interviewing a "young lady." She was a YouTuber on a weight loss journey. I call people Huns, Kins, and Love as signs of endearment. There is no harm or malice towards anyone given a nickname (or more).

Hun – That isn't just for a romantic partner. It has been a thing with me for years. I picked it up randomly. Like the almighty Source, God, or _____, it never left me.

Kins – As you can tell by your reading so far, I am a nerd. I roar about that proudly. One thing that I could remember was the Archie comics. I didn't read it heavily. As I got older, the Archieverse (as I would say) began to expand.

I remember Archie's Weird Mysteries. Archie's Weird Mysteries was a cartoon series. It aired here in New York City beginning in 1999 (on the UPN TV Network). I watched every episode before I went to school every day (I believe).

I noticed a brunette who had a crush on Archie. Her name was Veronica. She was known for calling Archie by her own nickname: Archiekins. I thought it was cool.

The cartoon would end after a season. The comics still went on. There would be a new Archie TV show called Riverdale (after I left my twenties). I watched a season or two. It was true to what I knew.

Veronica was in it. She did hang around Archie (like other characters). She did call him Archiekins.

I believe I started using Kins with my second fiancée. She didn't mind. It added to other names I had for her.

Laughs out loud

I eventually broke up with her. I stopped using Kins. It would be over a year until I called a woman by that name.

I went back to it (without a romantic partner). I wanted women to feel close to me. Not be reserved for whomever (graced me with being "my woman").

As you have seen, the most known Kins (in my life) is Blair Hayse. I called her that and never stopped. It has been over two years since that point. We're still friends to this day. I'm happy and grateful for this relationship.

Love – I've been a fan of Japanese culture since I was little. One thing was the actual Japanese language. I loved how different it was from English. I wouldn't really understand any of it until I was older.

I made time to try to learn it. I did the best I could. I watched Japanese media. I read a how-to-learn Japanese book. What I got was scrambled. Fortunately, I knew enough to translate.

This would unknowingly lead me to co-authoring with a woman named Mayuko. We met in a self-help course. We became friends outside of it. Mayu told me I can refer to her as Mayu Chan. Chan (in Japanese) means love.

I wound up calling someone else by Chan. I eventually went to the English version. Our friendship didn't last through the whole summer. I was lucky for what time I did have with her. I'm blessed she let me interview her, too.

As I recounted the Love bit, it took me back before I became a published author. I remember calling females by love as an adult. The biggest to receive that were my exes. Why? They were my loves.

I discussed the influence of self-help teachers. One thing I never forgot was what love really was. It really does begin with one person. That is yourself.

Enrolling in self-help courses. Releasing my exes from me. Reversing my diabetes. Becoming a published author. Keeping my jobs (as an adult). They were all forms of love.

The highest form of love given to us is called life. We are extensions of our true creator. We didn't breathe ourselves. Nor did our parents.

Letters of Love II

All it took was a "slow yes instead of a fast no" (to quote one Suzanne DePasse). I decided on my literary future. Putting material in the hands of a multiple-timed success. I wanted to have a story about my life from childhood through adulthood told.

They Are Magic was a very compelling book. I didn't know how big of a legacy it would give me. I really did feel like Dom Toretto. I got in my charger and then never stopped.

As you read, 2021 was quite a year for me. I transitioned from returning for a follow-up to doing two books (that eventually were published and released five days apart). Thank you for still reading this uncensored account of my life.

I recall being in *Letters of Magic*. I had already read *Ascension* by Jan Brent. I was doing my best to get into *Ascension Visionary Leaders* (or the overall Ascension series). I believe it had been two months with my new working schedule.

A former co-author (from *They Are Magic*) pings me. It was very unexpected. I didn't expect this person at all. That especially goes for their private nature.

We have an honest talk. We discuss our books, lives, etc. The person says,

"I notice you returned to Blair. Blair is doing a book called Letters of Magic. I have someone I'd like you to meet. I would like for you to talk to her."

I already had *Letters of Magic* on my plate. I was hoping to be in *Ascension*. I wasn't looking for a third book to be in. Plus, I was looking to get rid of my debt (as I shared earlier).

I would ping this woman. She seemed lovely looking. Had this nice vibe to her. She was from Sydney, Australia. Her name was Melissa Desveaux.

I set up to meet Melissa (Melly Love, as I eventually called her) on May 31st. We chatted on Zoom at 8:30 PM AEST. That is 6:30 AM EST. We spoke for about 30 minutes.

Our mutual friend pinged me. Did something uncharacteristic. What per se? Give me a bit of a pep talk. Said they were excited for us to talk.

The conversation went well. I thought Melly Love was a cute little hun. Loved how strong her accent was. She explained this book series she published.

I was won over. I signed up for *Letters of Love II* on the same day. That was the quickest of the four books to be paid for. I only had two payments. Got it done fully in a month.

I remember writing my letter was a challenge. I know Melly Love said that I could do two letters (if I wanted). I wanted a single one. That was enough.

At the time, my podcast was transitioning to its general third season. I found some brand-new podcasts. Some people had already joined me in BLK Lion's Domain.

I was still reeling from BLK Lion's Airspace not being monetized. I didn't completely love my primary income source being my only financial means. I never lost my passion for recording. I loved expressing myself.

This caused me to recall my podcast guesting days. I mentioned the Let's Voltron podcast birthed it. I loved people like my friends Datila, MGB Graham, and Matt Willis. Something kept rolling along, and then I found out who to write this letter to.

BLK Lion's Roar IV was born. I would bother Melissa regarding it. She ultimately told me that this was my letter. I'm digging very deep for this one. My podcasting foundations weren't just in my adult years.

I could see myself as a kid. A younger Zachary Shiloh Watts would mess with some of his father's tech. One piece of equipment was an actual microphone. I had no clue what that moment would do for me. I was just a goofball lad having fun.

Tribute to The Podcasting Community wasn't just to people I loved from it. It was a dedication to myself. I saw my growth in that industry. Not just there but across other industries as well.

Being in this book was more unique than *They Are Magic*, *Letters of Magic,* and *Ascension Visionary Leaders*. I never had a publisher interview me. Never had me join her on a Zoom call for YouTube distribution. I was used to interviewing my publisher (either before or after I joined a book). I loved being the recipient.

The interview took place on July 30, 2021. I remember it being up on a Wednesday morning. It was recorded at 6:30 AM EST. It was 8:30 PM for Melissa in Australia.

We talked about *BLK Lion's Roar IV*. Chatted about what was known as Love's Roar. There was something I didn't mention in this book (*In The Midst of CHAOS*).

I am not a highly political person. I never saw any differences between Democrats and Republicans (here in America). They were more influential Bloods and Crips gangs. Both sides want the same things (in their own terms).

I love people. I really do. If I love you, I will go out of my way to do something for ya. Melly Desveaux was one person. She kept posting about a dream she had. The other authors shared her sentiments.

The *Letters of Love II* family wanted one Michelle Obama. What did they want her for? They believed our book would garner more attention (if the only non-Caucasian first-American lady wrote our forward).

I was at work for the majority of my day on July 27, 2021. I recalled having some downtime. I thought, *"Okay. I am not political, but I believe in the power of dreams. These women are passionate about our book. Why not?"*

I wrote out a letter to Mrs. Obama. I thought about not just the whole *Letters of Love II* lot. I thought of my parents (who loved the heck out of her and her hubby). That letter came quicker than all four BLK Lion's Roars.

I wasn't getting my hopes up. I was trying to talk to the wife of a historical politician. She gets many messages asking for stuff. I didn't get myself all worked up.

I didn't receive a hello. It sucked for those who didn't get what they wanted from the group. This was like trying to have Santa Claus stay for dinner and then getting your heart broken (when he is a no-show). My heart goes out over a year later.

You're asking, *"Do you regret writing your letter to Mrs. Obama?"* No, I don't. What is the last word in this letter's series? Love.

I would do it again. Why? I loved all who hoped for Mrs. Obama. That was a motivation for me. I needed no other reason than that.

Love is a beautiful thing. Mine rewarded me. I got several opportunities. Two revolved in BLK Lion's Domain.

Remember the launch day for *Ascension Visionary Leaders*? One of those authors returned for this book series. I got to talk with Veronica Sanchez De Darivas. She wasn't just in *Letters of Love* and my previous book. She had her own book called: *21 Habits: Positive Words*.

I bought both books on August 8, 2021. I honored her request to do her solo book daily for a week. She loved that I enjoyed her work. When Veronica was interviewed by me, it wasn't long. We chatted for less than an hour.

Please listen here:

[BLK Lion's Airspace Episode 517 - Universal Grounding in BLK Lion's Domain with Veronica Sanchez by BLK Lion's Airspace (anchor.fm)](#)

The other BLK Lion's Domain was with Melly Love herself. She suggested we go on what was *"Zachary Shiloh Around the World"* day. We didn't just talk about the forthcoming book. Our thirty-minute chat was about the *Letters of Love* legacy, her background, my letter to Michelle Obama, and much more.

Please listen here:

[BLK Lion's Airspace Episode 534 - Universal Grounding in BLK Lion's Domain with Melissa Desveaux by BLK Lion's Airspace (anchor.fm)](#)

The book launch date was October 10, 2021. It was on a Sunday. How do I remember this? I was with my surrogate dad (during a televised Catholic church service). Plus, I recall what I ate that day.

It started with an actual launch party. I woke up just as that was going on. I joined after I took my shower. At the request of a certain someone, I put on a familiar hat. It was for branding purposes.

The Zoom call was over. I did what I did for the previous three launches. I promoted, promoted, promoted. It was fun interacting with authors as I hustled.

Zachary Shiloh's Letter to Michelle Obama

Published in its original form

July 27, 2021

Dear Mrs. Michelle Obama:

How are you? I hope all is well. Thank you for reading this letter.

My name is Zachary Shiloh Watts. I am a co-author of a forthcoming book called Letters of Love II. The book is being released on October 10, 2021.

Why am I writing this letter to you?

I am contacting you on behalf of my publisher named Melissa Desveaux. Melly Love (as I call her) would love for you to write the forward to our book. Not just Melly. The rest of the Letters of Love II family would feel blessed by your presence (as well).

Letters of Love II is the fourth co-authoring I am part of this year. The previous three I was featured in were majority co-authored by Americans. I had no problem with that at all. Why I am American myself.

This is very special to me. I am not surrounded by majority Americans in the Letters of Love II family. I represent

America by myself. I see your blessing as an opportunity to strengthen America's relationships with other countries (such as Australia and the United Kingdom).

The books (I have written chapters) have been unisex compilations. The authors were mainly women. I didn't mind that fact. I was fortunate to co-authored with three other men. Every outing was very fun to participate in.

What I loved most about the writings was that they encouraged people. This was especially powerful from the female standpoint. Your appearance would empower women around the world to live their dreams.

Speaking of dreams, I think of my own mother. I come from an all-African American family. I know how much it meant to her and my father to see your husband become American President 13 years ago.

Her support has meant a lot to me. It has since I was old enough to walk. The Letters of Love II forward be another historic moment for my mother. I'm sure she'd never forget that for the rest of her life. Her son introduced in a book (with his writing family) by the only African American First Lady.

I don't know what the future holds. I'm happy and grateful to get a response. I understand if you decline writing the forward. From the bottom of my heart, I thank you for your consideration.

God bless you. Please take care yourself and your loved ones.

Respectfully,

Zachary Shiloh Watts

The BLK Lion's Roars Become Disorganized

Sometime after I got into *Letters of Love II*, I was offered to be in a different book. Try being part of something that didn't have a very good footing. Try having your patience tested like you never had before. Try handling massive writer's block (that was worse than when you started writing your original story).

Try not having good communication with your publisher for months. Try controlling your anger as you learn the foreword writer talked to the publisher (more than you). Try sitting idle as this free (to join) "passion project" was going nowhere. Try pushing yourself to stay (where you sensed you should leave).

Try being pinged by an editor (who had no clue) about what was going on. Try being in disbelief when you talked to two of your co-authors (regarding how long they have waited). Add on more anger when you find out how long this general book was being born.

Try being sympathetic when the husband of your main publisher dies. Try having hope that this compilation will be released (before your following two books). Try watching your relationship with someone who was in three writing families (as you) perish (as the next year approaches).

Try containing yourself as your BLK Lion's Roars get out of order. Try explaining why there isn't a home for *BLK Lion's Roar V*. Try to find a blessing (or more) literally In The Midst of CHAOS.

Magical Miracles

Doesn't matter if animal, human, or whatever. Everything (on Earth) has a beginning. For every start, there's an end.

Blair Hayse returned to BLK Lion's Domain on August 28, 2021. It's been nearly a year since we produced one of the highest-grossing episodes of my podcast. Blair shocked me more in this than in the previous. I didn't expect her back so quick.

If Blairkins returned, I thought it would be closer to this live event she wanted to do. Wanted to do are the main words. I was happy and grateful to get this second interview. Made the general day more memorable.

So we were fresh from *Letters of Magic* nearly for four weeks. It was great to talk about the road to our book. We chatted about *They Are Magic*. We discussed general life leading to the day we were interviewing for.

As the episode gets ready to wrap up, I mention that my mentor made an announcement (on Facebook). The Magic series family of books was coming to a close. She had one more left. It was called *Magical Miracles*.

Blair spoke about it in private with me a smidge. I heard her reasonings. I didn't question her one bit. A- she was heading back to Corporate America. B- wanted more time with her family. C- our beloved Flowtastic Angel wasn't around anymore.

The greatest for me was to honor Jenn Kirch. As I said, she wasn't just a writer. She wasn't just an editor. Jenn was our hype woman. I applauded Blair.

Please listen to the interview here:

[BLK Lion's Airspace Episode 526 - Universal Grounding in BLK Lion's Domain with Blair Hayse by BLK Lion's Airspace (anchor.fm)](anchor.fm)

I was in every unisex book by Blair Hayse Publishing. When Blair made her announcement, others expected me to return. BHP was my main writing home for nearly a year. Why not have their most recognized guy in the finale?

I definitely wasn't missing *Magical Miracles*. I made my name in the Magic series. It was right for me to be in it. I would say it's my birthright. I think Blair herself was hoping I'd join her in saying goodbye.

I was hoping some co-Magic authors I had would return. Nobody from *They Are Magic* or *Letters of Magic* returned. Nearly everyone (I was close to) had transitioned from writing to whatever else they were passionate about (such as public speaking and coaching). If they did write, then they were going solo.

As with every Magic book, Blair did get some human beings on board. The Magic family for our farewell was mostly new. Six new faces, to be exact. Three were non-Magic series, best-selling authors. One was a successful solo writer.

Rounding out the veterans were Mayuko Fukino and Karen Quiros. I believe that Karebear brought two new authors for Blairkins. I had two on my end. My two were from *Letters of Love II*.

I am sure she must have heard this (not just from me). *"Blair Hayse, you gotta end a magic book (with yourself) one day."* Blair talked with me (in private) about writing. She is a very humble woman. Felt that all (who were in the last chapter) had a more powerful story.

I didn't tell Blairkins that to kiss her ass. The Magic series wasn't written in alphabetical order. If that was the case, I would have been the end (in every single book we did). Blairkins was worthy of the last slot by storytelling.

Magical Miracles was nearly two years in the making. Not because it's the end of an empowering series. Blair Hayse finally took her rightful spot to finish. I said it to her on launch. I will again.

I couldn't see anyone else ending...

Not me. Not the New York City blondes. Not the cousins from *Letters of Love II*. Not Mayuko. Not Danielle. Not Magnolia.

Blair was the beginning of the Magic series (just with her vision). She was in every book that her company published. It was the right choice. That's my opinion. Others agreed with me.

We did the Zoom call. All involved were excited for the day ahead. We were told to take care of ourselves and thanked for being in the book.

Once the call finished, we had some goals. Have fun with each other. Promote the book to the top spot (across all chosen charts).

Simple things to do, right? This day wasn't just memorable for good only. Something awful happened.

We live in a highly digital world. We have different means of networks. Financially by banks. Television. News. Social media.

I have been a part of several launch days for books (as you have just read). They all had a common factor. We had amazon.com as a distributor. Those days were for the e-book version. So, we had people buy for Kindle (or digital devices that have the same outlet).

Amazon is the world's biggest retailer. How do I know? I'm not just a published author there. When *Magical Miracles* was released, I was an Amazon employee for over a year.

I don't know how, but Amazon was really messed up that day. I didn't know it. I don't watch the news (nor have I yearned to do so). I was focused entirely (on *Magical Miracles*). I did what I absolutely did best.

Blair (as per launch days) kept us aware of things. I could sense the new (more so than returning) authors were worried. It wasn't just with our book. This was a worldwide crisis taking place.

I don't know why. I never stopped believing in *Magical Miracles* (as we had worldly troubles). *Magical Miracles* wasn't only a book name. Lived beyond a cliché. It was in our hearts.

It was our desires manifested. A group of women (with a man) together as one family. Our lives are brought to the forefront for other human beings to consume. It was months in the making.

Zachary Shiloh Watts was present. This was his fifth book launch and his co-authoring finale for 2021. He wanted it to be as successful as he could.

I believe I showed not just my promotional power. I asserted myself as a leader. I wasn't letting a huge problem kill what momentum we had. I wanted all co-authors to keep hope alive.

Not to give up because it seemed our book was stuck. That just us staying on course would get what we wanted. Love, passion, and purpose would reward us. The rest of the launch day was moving as if the Amazon crash never existed.

I returned to work on December 8, 2021. Told of what happened in the actual Amazon warehouse (where I was really employed). Moved forward in my life there. Did my absolute best as the Amazon Peak season was "wrapping up."

As I headed to work on December 9, 2021, I saw an announcement from Blair Hayse. Blairkins said that *Magical Miracles* hit #1. It was such on several book charts. Hit the international status in numerous countries.

As I wrap up this story, it makes me think of a different book. One that had limitless potential. A masterpiece that wasn't published by Blair Hayse, DarkQuarks Publishing, or Melissa Desveaux. You can read about it another time.

Rebel Romance

Rebel Romance meant a lot to Zachary Shiloh. It wasn't just a sextacular. It wasn't prototypical smut. It was a reality changer.

breathes

My journey with it began before the October 2021 official start date. It began, I would say, maybe a month after *They Are Magic* was released. I met this beautiful woman from Poland. She resided in Scotland.

Her name was Sandra. Sandy is the other half of DarkQuarks Publishing. She is a multi-time best-selling author. She was a co-author of *Ascension Visionary Leaders.*

We messaged each other on Facebook. I loved our interactions. I swear it was like talking to a more successful version of Zachary Shiloh.

Sometime after I met Sand, Janet Brent joined me for *Universal Grounding in BLK Lion's Domain.* It was the same episode where Jan discussed *Ascension* with me. It was more memorable for two reasons.

We were both jonesing out for Sandy. We were her biggest fans. We loved her laugh. We enjoyed her general presence. That was especially true for me.

Janet teased something she was working on. I thought it was an invite to read a collection of her naughty tales. When I say naughty, I mean stuff for Erotica. She told me this book was called *Rebel Romance*.

I didn't think I'd be in an Erotica. I had my share of romances. Witness countless acts of sex in movies and television. Me? No form, shape, or way I thought I was in *Rebel Romance*.

I imagined how cool it would be. Adding a different genre to my author list. Getting out of my comfort zone. Being part of a first-ever book.

I kept talking to Sandra (when I could). I felt like I was high as a kite. Every conversation was lively (or so I thought they were). I eventually grew a crush on her.

A light bulb sparked. I found my erotic muse. I joined *Rebel Romance* on June 5, 2021. I wanted to tell the world about my Unforgettable Polish Love.

I began writing what I hoped to be the legit seventh BLK Lion's Roar in August 2021. My writing style went from wildfire to INFERNO. I was writing about my beloved Sand multi-dimensionally. The number one woman (I thought in my mind).

Polish Love got me through maybe one of the roughest months (in the Coronavirus Pandemic). Fueled me to not take time off from work. Made seconds into minutes. Minutes into hours.

Before I knew it, I was ready for the official start. I handed *My Unforgettable Polish Love* to Janet Brent. I believe the real-life Polish Love herself, too. I was excited for them to read it.

DarkQuarks Publishing did a three-day Erotica event. It was from September 15th to the 17th, 2021. I was there for two days. The only day I missed live was the middle.

I never forgot the finale. We attendees meditated with our hosts. Did some actual journal writing (for an x amount of time). I was called to speak.

I looked my Polish Love in her eyes. Made it known how much I admired her. Proclaimed she would be the greatest BLK Lion's Roar. I believe she was touched by what I said.

Sandra did join me in BLK Lion's Domain. We talked about her book called *Leap Afraid*. I lived that book to the fullest. I put a blazer on for her. I spoke to Polish Love in full color.

Please listen here:

[BLK Lion's Airspace Episode 530 - Universal Grounding in BLK Lion's Domain with Sandra Stachowicz by BLK Lion's Airspace (anchor.fm)](#)

Each author had their announcement by Janet (as we eventually got to *Rebel Romance* start). Mine was right before the Polish Love mini-tour. When it came, I was hyped. I did my own as well.

I was excited to build for the road to launch. We had guest teachers for Erotica-based workshops. The authors interacted with me on Facebook. The energy felt right to us all.

The book launch path wasn't completely positive. I had been in touch with Janet Brent the majority of the time. Would ask her about things. We were friends for a about a year.

I mentioned this during *Ascension Visionary Leaders*. I loved Jan because she wasn't only a co-author. Not just one-half of my publishers. She was our editor.

Things started to sour when she told me that she wasn't editing *Rebel Romance*. I wasn't heated. My jaw was on the floor. I couldn't believe what I read. It was the truth, though. No bullshit.

We moved forward with production. The Zoom classes were fun. I'm thinking we are full steam ahead.

Buzzer sound effect

I was totally wrong.

We had deadlines. Drafts were due on specific dates. They were missed. I dismissed it because of the words *"schedule subject to change."*

It got worse. *Rebel Romance* began getting delayed further. I believe it was stalled for almost a month. I was already handling the book that fucked up the order of my seven BLK Lion's Roars. I wasn't thrilled with another problem.

I was considering leaving *Rebel Romance*. I didn't like being kept in the dark. It triggered me hotter with Polish Love. When she was around, she was very avoidant.

I am happy and grateful because I wasn't only talking to the five-foot-two-inch goofball squad. The non-publishing co-authors conversed with me. Some had the *"Let it play out"* mentality. Others were like me with the *"This is bullshit"* mindset.

What did I love in the midst of that time? All parties involved were passionate. We wanted *Rebel Romance* released. Ready to arouse our audiences. Join our Romantic Rebellion (as we launch).

Those of us (who were upset) did make posts. Me? I was insulted. I wound up losing interviews for my podcast. The book seemed like it didn't see the light of day. As the only male author, I wouldn't sit on the sidelines.

I laid in thick about how I felt (on January 3, 2022). I felt as if the DarkQuarks Publishing team didn't respect us authors. We cared about them (and our editor) as human beings. If one (or all) was sick, then let us know.

We changed from one male editor to a non-Janet Brent female. Left one release date to one that the majority agreed fit more perfectly. Promotions were building hype for the book strongly.

The undisputed launch date for *Rebel Romance* was February 14, 2022. This was cool to see. My general sixth book was out on the most romantic day of the year.

No pre promo Zoom call. An abundance container fell out of my pocket (then broke) the night before. I was feeling blessed regardless. I was up prior to sunrise. Kept my book launch tradition of reading what I was in.

A majority of stories never left me. They were arousing with some sex involved. I can give some themes I noticed.

There was supernaturality. We had worldwide travel. We had romantic soulmates. Talked about food relationships. Hybrids from fake to real stories.

I told all of the authors my thoughts. I had no filter to me. I meant every single word.

We promoted the book for the majority of the day. There was a midday Zoom call in America. Any non-Americans were in the early morning or night time. We celebrated our material.

I talked about my journey. My happiness and gratitude for the day. Giving a non-spoiler review of the compilation. My excitement to promote.

After the call wrapped, it was back to getting that baby to the top spot. I kept going. Made my unique posts. Tagged all the authors I had. Etc, etc.

I took care of other things in my life. Wrapped up the promotion on my end the next morning. The girls did the rest. Mission accomplished.

Dare To Dream

Blair Hayse appeared on my *BLK Lion's Airspace* podcast twice. There was something I left out in her second run. I am sharing it right here.

Blair announced that not only was she ending the Magic series. *Magical Miracles* was her company's final book under the name of Blair Hayse Publishing. We were heading into a new era.

It is Fall 2021. It is late November. Your mentor has taken to Facebook following Thanksgiving. The Almighty Blairkins has announced the first book she's publishing in 2022. The first book for Elite Publishing House is called *Dare to Dream*.

Your name is Zachary Shiloh Watts. You are still in a book that contained your fifth BLK Lion's Roar. You went on to interview your only male publisher (for the technical second time). Not just him but his publishing partner and some of your fellow co-authors.

You were trying to be hopeful about the present you are living. You had goals you wanted to accomplish. You kept fighting against the negative you saw. Your fifth BLK Lion's Roar isn't released before your sixth.

You head into 2022, not completely satisfied. You get into the new year. You make it halfway through January with your *BLK Lion's Roar V* homeless.

I was looking for a home. I knew of a goal I had. I always kept in touch with Blair. I signed up for a different book she hoped to do.

It would go nowhere. People weren't signing up. That really bothered me a bit. Not so much that I wanted to punch a wall. Usually, when Blair starts a new book, there would be a positive attraction for the venture.

I wound up eventually joining *Dare to Dream*. The date was January 29, 2022. I knew someone was in the book. Unknown told me in an interview. Blair wanted no drama.

I said *"Don't bother, Blairkins. This is a different playing field. You are running the show. When you're in charge, shit gets done. We go gold."*

I know that took a lot of pressure off her. We had goals in mind. This was something to bring us closer to our visions. Not only that, but my precious *BLK Lion's Roar V* finally had an undisputed home.

I officially announce that I am in *Dare to Dream* on February 6th, 2022. It was eight days before *Rebel Romance* launched. Ten days prior to *They Are Magic* being a year old. I didn't announce it on my actual sign date because I believe I didn't know what to say.

I mentioned this in my actual chapter intro (for *Dare to Dream*), but it's worth the repeat. I asked Blair what was *Dare to Dream* about. Could I write as if I had accomplished some dreams? Blairkins simply said, *"It's your journey to a dream."*

This caused me to really dig deep. I began writing after my birthdate. It's amazing that I turned 35 years of age one day after my *Dare to Dream* signing. I still smile at that.

I had many dreams growing up. I thought of the biggest one that I was living. I am still living it. I would talk about how I got out of Madison Square Garden with my family. Helped out a gentleman with $5.00 so he could live another day.

I wrote about how it helped me grow up. I simply wanted to help people. I still do so multidimensionally to this day. My podcast. My writings. Much more…

The months flew by. Some people were concerned for my well-being. Why? Another shooting occurred during springtime. A co-author contacted me via phone call.

I had no clue what was going on. I was at work when that tragedy happened. I don't follow the news. The biggest thing about that day was I had my cell phone off. At work, I am not playing on my phone all day.

I made my phone call. I told her (co-author) that I was okay. Had my friend relay to Blair and an Elite Publishing alum that I was okay. Said that I would message each. I kept my word and then moved forward.

Craziness is part of the world we live in. I would feel it from my own family. I was agitated in late spring. Will not go into heavy details. Let's just say I am still coping with certain actions.

I got all of my edits in. Got my promotional pictures. Hyped the book on Facebook (ala Instagram). Did whatever else was required of me.

We make it to June 14, 2022. It is launch day. You know my tradition for the day. Let's add a pinch of difference. Shall we? To quote one Ace Ventura Pet Detective, *"Alrighty then."*

So I read the book. History repeats itself order wise. I'm not complaining. I am right between the other non-Caucasians again. This time went man, woman, man, woman.

We get to the final chapters. It warmed my heart when it happened in *Magical Miracles*. Doing it in reverse to usher in Elite Publishing House's first book was something I didn't foresee. Not at all.

Blair Hayse was the second to last chapter. Mayuko Fukino-Mayhill was the finale. What better way to introduce Elite than the two women from *She Is Magic, Always*. I couldn't think of anyone else.

Did the Zoom call with Blair and whomever else. Went out to promote. Did other things throughout my day. Went to bed that evening feeling pleased.

Zachary Shiloh is Overcome by Overwhelm

It's circa January to February 2022. Your BLK Lion's Roars have been put into CHAOS. Your fifth BLK Lion's Roar was homeless. You're approached by the former editor of an aforementioned book.

She tells you how good you are. How much better this would be than where you were. You'd have a stronger network.

You've been used to writing in co-authorings. You had been an opening chapter. You were featured midway a few times. You were the finale of two books (in your first appearance for two different series).

This new venture puts you at a level you never had. You're not a main chapter writer. You are an interlude writer. Your job is to set someone up.

The book's theme overall is about overwhelm. You know what overwhelm is like. You feel it around you. You see the sensation. You hear it practically every day.

You take your time to just flush it out. You talk about the loss of friends. You are going somewhere you initially had no plans to be part of. You mention your sexuality. You discuss being a coach for free.

How you felt that you were stuck. How you lived on prayers. How you weathered these problems. Before you know it, you've finished your chapter. You send it with your bio to your publisher.

You have been used to having an actual direction. Your previous publishers had a set schedule of dates. You knew when they would do Facebook Lives. You would have Q&A sessions. You knew when your book would be released.

What if you finally didn't have any of that? What if you felt lost? What if you were uncertain about the book being released this year?

Winter becomes spring in mere months. You have a definite home for *BLK Lion's Roar V*. It's not this book you're in. You feel happy and grateful.

The month you are in is precisely May. You get notified that the book has officially launched. Your mind is blown. You don't know how to react. You tell former co-authors that your new material has been released.

You are looking for help and they give it to you. Their support takes off some of this edge. You do your best to promote it all day. When the day is done, you go to bed.

You wake up the very next morning. You go on amazon.com to view how you did. You see, this thing is at a particular position. You feel it can do better.

You go to two women. Both have co-authored with ya. You have done such two times (or more). You go to them seeking advice. How can we make this thing move?

Each tells you basically the same. You read their words in Facebook Messenger. You can hear their respective voices (in your head). You love, appreciate, and value their unified opinion.

You take this to your publisher. A co-author basically says no. The publisher agrees with the individual. You go back to work promoting. You do your best.

You stop briefly to go buy your parents a newspaper. Not just for the biological family do you make the purchase. This helps get you out of the house for a bit. It lets you interact with other human beings without words (being typed on a screen).

You return to where you live. You take your shower. You're feeling relaxed. You are ready to promote the book again.

When you head back to Facebook, nothing is being done. Your anger peaks to its maximum. You make your opinion known. You leave during what is supposed to be your second day of launch.

This would unknowingly bleed into a book that you would return to. You are overwhelmed yet stand In The Midst of CHAOS. You thank yourself. You thank your true friends. You get rid of what you felt was dead weight.

Breathes…

Being A Best-Selling Author

New York Times?

Los Angeles Times?

Barnes and Noble?

Amazon?

It is something I never thought I wanted. Something I didn't know I'd aspire to be. Something that I unknowingly would achieve more than once. That is being a best-selling author.

Each of my best sellers meant a lot to me. I still remember all of the eight. I could have talked about them in their respective points, but I wanted a special section.

As you read, February 16, 2021, was the date that *They Are Magic* was released. I remember when Blair Hayse announced that we went best seller. The feeling was incredible. It was humbling to be along with my mentor as she obtained her general sixth.

I thought I was the only first-time best-seller there. I was used to Blair having numerous returns. Said authors get another with her. I was happily wrong.

Joining me in the single-timer's lane were two women. The first was my guest for BLK Lion's Domain (after Universal

Grounding started taking place). That was Stephanie Mahony. We talked about being in *They Are Magic*.

The other was Tammy Lambrou. Tammy Love joined me in BLK Lion's Domain, too. She continues to live her life as a mother and volleyball coach.

Not many joined Blair for a return. They felt one time was good enough. I respected that along the way. I always will do so.

The 2X time is a rare breed of writers. *Letters of Magic* was my introduction to it. I wasn't the only two-time best-seller produced. Three of my co-authors joined that prestigious group.

Tammy Love achieved this feat. I am blown away by her. She was like me. We both got ours in the Magic unisex books. We did so in two books straight.

Geneva Hill (under the name of Eve) earned hers here. I laugh that she used a false name. If you read her story, then I believe you can see why she did such.

Brooke Coleman. My beloved Purr Hun. She can that she was in two magic books straight. The last real *She Is Magic*. The second-ever Magic unisex.

Ascension Visionary Leaders was my first best-seller without Blair. My first as the only male in a book. My first as the only black person (in the DarkQuarks Publishing Ascension series). The first in a majority non-Caucasian book. My first in a majority UK writer-based book.

Ascension would be the book that would inspire me. It gave me a dream. As I mentioned earlier, I had a crush on a woman (who went on to be my romantic counterpart in *Rebel Romance*). I wanted to match her in best-selling authorships. It even brought a desire to exceed her.

Ascension gave me some more firsts. It was my first best-seller with DarkQuarks Publishing. It was my first co-authoring with my friend Veronica Sanchez De Darivas.

Letters of Love II saw my return to the two-times club. It was my second best-seller without Blair Hayse. My second in a majority non-Caucasian book. Second, as the only male (in a general book). It gave me my second as a letter writer.

Letters of Love II marked a first-time occasion. I was taught about tagging other people. It helps with registering things on social media. For example, say you want a book called *Letters of Love II*? You can see numerous posts about that book.

I tagged my co-authors in three books straight (as you read). What if I told you *Letters of Love II* was where I never tagged anyone? That I promoted this book alone (on my end)? That I only reacted to and commented on my co-authors' posts?

I can say that I tagged nobody for one book. Why? Remember the woman I call My Unforgettable Polish Love?

She noticed me. I was known for tagging people (outside of book promotions). I tagged not to give people power over me (as Polish Love assumed). I felt that I was helping others. Saying, *"Hey! _____ is doing this or, we're working together on _____ ".*

I decided to take that goofball woman's challenge. I did so prior to the *Letters of Love II* launch. It was interesting to be on a launch where I used no tags. I showed my power. I was strong without tagging.

It did garner attention from the *Letters of Love II* writers. They were so used to me tagging them (before Polish Love called me out). They loved how inclusive I was. How passionate I was about our book. I wanted that baby to be a best-seller.

I helped them, but they missed me. Tagging was a helpful tool. I would eventually go back to it. I would have my moments where I tagged no one. *Letters of Love II* gave me such a wonderful opportunity.

If my beloved Polish Love ever read this, I thank her for giving me the challenge.

Magical Miracles was my first earned through leadership. The first of the disorganized BLK Lion's Roars. My general fifth best seller.

Rebel Romance is my general sixth. "The proper seventh." I am in awe of this one the most. As I got into gear to write this best-seller section (you're reading now), I felt a rush of emotions.

When it genuinely happened, I was in awe that I unknowingly tied with a publisher. I read a good wad of her stuff. For me to tie with Janet Brent in best-sellers was a cool feeling.

I am a naughty guy. I can be a bit of a flirt. I admit that proudly. I did that on my podcast. I have done such in conversations.

I smile brightly that this was my first Erotica. To be a first-time best-seller in this genre was mind-blowing. It justified that sex can be power. It showed me that I could channel my naughty side into a successful writing.

All of the books I did (from *They Are Magic* through *Magical Miracles*) were clean. I never cussed in a book. There was only one of the seven BLK Lion's Roars that got me to use dirty language. *Rebel Romance* was it.

I was already a rebel. Why not break the paradigm? Make people's jaws drop? Embrace myself fully by saying fuck, shit, ass, and more. *Rebel Romance* is the only foul language best-selling book that Zachary Shiloh Watts did this in.

Rebel gave me another powerful thing in best sellers. I mirrored my biggest mentor, Blair Hayse. Blairkins became a 6X best-selling author in February 2021 (as I mentioned). How do I reflect her?

When was *Rebel Romance* released? It was in February 2022. I gained my sixth best with it.

I not only tied with Janet Brent in best-sellers, but I did have the same number of best-sellers as Blair in the month of February.

Dare To Dream was the last BLK Lion's Roar to be a best-seller. It was my first best with Elite Publishing House (after their transitioning from Blair Hayse Publishing). It was the finale to catch up to My Unforgettable Polish Love.

I talked about my teachers in the self-help world through this book. They helped shape me into the man I am today. I wouldn't have written this without their teachings. I am humbled and grateful to reveal another thing *Dare to Dream* did.

As I began My Unforgettable Polish Love to tie with my *Rebel Romance* counterpart, I noticed something. Shall I really say a specific someone? One of the most prominent self-help teachers is Marianne Williamson.

Marianne had published thirteen books. She is a numerous time best-selling author. Of those books, she had seven best-sellers. *Dare to Dream* tied Zachary Shiloh Watts with this legendary figure in best-selling authorships.

I repeatedly mentioned Dominic Toretto as my favorite *Fast and Furious* character. I talked about how he got in his Dodge Charger. There was a quote that he had in the same film. After Dom wins the first street race (of the motion picture), he says:

"Ask any racer. Any real racer. It doesn't matter if it's an inch or a mile. Winning is winning".

The quote I used above didn't really hit me until August 2022. I thought a book (I was in) failed. I laid it out in the *Zachary Shiloh is Overcome by Overwhelm* chapter. I learned in a discussion with Blair Hayse that I was an 8X best-selling author. I'm still shocked to this day by that.

I was used to being in seven #1 best-selling books. The unnamed book was a 95 on a book chart. I'll talk about that in a different book.

As I continued writing this book, I remembered I was around best-selling authors (before I was friends with any). I was a geeky kid. As you've read this book, you know that I became a nerdy adult. One of my loves was Pro Wrestling. I was a huge fan for over 20 years.

One of my favorite Pro Wrestlers was Dwayne "The Rock" Johnson. He was the coolest non-Caucasian I saw in the World Wrestling Federation. He spoke then crowds would listen (regardless of boos or cheers). He was the guy that I used frequently in video games. As I got older, I would play some of his in-ring interviews a lot.

Doing this book alone made me remember a stat that some may forget. The Rock was a best-selling author. He added this title with his autobiography called *The Rock Says*. It is a great feeling to know that I have a title shared with this successful man.

Why Co-Author?

I repeatedly mentioned how I was looking to improve myself. How I learned from some of the most prominent teachers. A reminder that I was taught by Sonia Ricotti. Sonia wasn't only known for her Unsinkable system.

In early 2020, I watched a documentary by my teacher. She interviewed some of her best friends. One happened to be Dr. John Gray. He is the author of *Men Are From Mars, Women Are From Venus.* He talks about how his wife named, Bonnie, influenced him.

Mrs. Gray died in 2018. Dr. Gray discussed how she was on her deathbed. He was apologizing to his wife for not giving her credit toward his book series. After she passed away, it ate at him that he never put her as his co-author.

That touched me to my soul. I believe that some part of me wished I could be a co-author. Be with a woman who was featured in books. I had no clue (in a non-romantic relationship) that what I was hoping for manifested. I had no idea that it would be exactly eight times.

Nor thought that I would be with a woman. I got to be with numerous women. Some were repeats from books I was in. Many would-be one-shot deals.

Age is a number. So are book appearances. I am happy and grateful to be in the same space with these souls.

Going Solo

When I think of my writing career, I feel like a person in the music industry. I mentioned myself as a lesser-known Michael Jackson. When people think of Michael Jackson, they think of him as the pipsqueak lead singer of the Jackson Five. I think of him as an adult who had hit albums such as Off the Wall, Thriller, and Bad.

The Jacksons: *An American Dream* showed him from birth through The Victory Tour. You were able to understand him. Why he is the man he was. Why he was successful. See his pain, sorrow, and joy. Same with his other siblings.

It didn't take me years to want to do my own stuff. I wanted to do *BLK Lion's Roar* as a solo book. I went nowhere with it to the point that I sought help. I channeled myself through the connections I had. Got featured in four books. Rest, as you saw, was history.

What you don't know is when the solo bug really manifested. I was successful on the co-authoring tip for almost six months. *They Are Magic*, *Letters of Magic,* and *Ascension Visionary Leaders* have already been published. I am a 3X best-selling author. I am waiting for *Letters of Love II* (so I can obtain my fourth).

I felt like Alexander the Great. I heard his story in different outlets. The freshest account came from a Pro Wrestling documentary. It was for Brock Lesnar.

Brock Lesnar is one of the most iconic figures in World Wrestling Entertainment history. He arrived on the WWE main roster in 2002. He became the youngest WWE Champion in August that year.

In the 2003 release called *Here Comes the Pain*, Paul Heyman (Brock's on-screen manager and lawyer) used the story of Alexander the Great to describe Brock. How did it go? The mythological figure had defeated all of his foes. He came to a point where he wept for his future.

I did the co-authoring multiple times. I was chasing my Polish Love in best-sellers. I thought to myself, *"Where do I go from here? I could write with Blairkins, DarkQuarks, and Melly Love forever. I am a best-selling author. I could be a 7X by year's end."*

I remembered the women I had interviewed in BLK Lion's Domain. I had Dr. Lemuria Nesbitt in the springtime. Talked with Veronica Sanchez De Darivas (who was waiting for *Letters of Love II*, too) in August. I chatted with Marquetta LaRae and Stephanie Mahony after *Goddess Rising* was released (in early October 2021). I believe that Blairkins herself mentioned solo writing (in our second podcast round).

As I heard these huns above, I felt a calling. Time flew with each interview. The calling wasn't via a phone. Didn't brew on a Zoom call. It grew in my heart (like being a Holistic Health Coach, doing my podcast, and whatever else I was passionate about).

I found that the call was to go solo. All of the mentioned were successful in co-authoring. They had (or were making) their own solo book. I thought, *"Why not me?"*

Other people were encouraging me to be on my own. They gave me reasons to do this venture. This would be an opening for me. Allowed me to celebrate the life I lived. The possibility of my publishers not doing co-authoring books (after fruitful launches) increased.

I did invest in a publishing course by Melly Desveaux. We met once a week for a month. We had one other person live. There was one other, but she was in the UK. She valued getting her sleep.

I wound up not doing my own publishing. That didn't mean I wasn't for solo bookwork. As you have read, things do come together. It just takes time.

Mind Over Matter Unlimited

It began with a desire. My desire to be a Holistic Health Coach. I was reflecting on my writing career. How I got to spring 2022.

I was feeling a tug on my heart (similar to becoming a solo book writer). Not in a bad way. I felt that I was meant to be something more. There was a real purposeful work for me.

Interactions with people (such as my biological father) showed me that I wasn't completely happy. I had friends who were doing what they loved. They had careers such as bank tellers, realtors, and more. Not just living their dream lives but getting paid for their services rendered.

I paid my share of money for self-help improvements. It may had been for just mindset. Maybe me supporting the people I loved. I worked on myself so hard that people asked why am I not making money (from what I love).

I let go of myself. I became increasingly busy. I was trying to keep a job for income (more than a sense of pleasure). I felt like a failure (for months on end).

Why should I be paid? Why should I be compensated for nothing? We live in a world where results make a difference. You've seen it reading my co-authoring journeys.

All of this is part of why I took a sabbatical. I worked my ass off for my employer. I was getting paid for something that made me miserable at times. I wasn't manifesting coaching clients there (when this rest period was birthing itself). Blessedly, I made it over 18 months in such a concrete jungle.

I was gifted time off from April 27th to May 16, 2022. The road to my vacation saw me surrounded by resurrection. I was sitting outside one day when Resurrection (Paper, Paper, Paper) by Bone Thugs "N" Harmony played in a car (that passed me by). I could hear the song called *"Resurrection Rap"* by a Christian singer named Carmen (as well).

I took those songs as signs to get my shit together. I thought about what was a coming three-year journey. One that wasn't only weight loss. I was losing my life.

When I was dying from my unknown diabetes, I knew I wasn't right in my head. I was a fairly optimistic guy. My personality was fucked up for nearly a year. As you saw, I made quite a life. I was serious about not just mine. I cared for others as well.

As you have read, I play with words. They have led to my BLK Lion's Roars being formed. Helped me to transition my BLK Lion's Domain (from Roaming Around to Universal Grounding). This was no different from making the Mind Over Matter Unlimited mission statement.

I asked myself, *"What would Zachary Shiloh Watts really say? What would I do?"* The first thing is to become highly energetic. Be welcoming to all who I talked to.

Two keywords I kept hearing were health resurrection. Health resurrection is my mission. To deny what I am generally about is a lie.

We, human beings, are manifesting every single day. We do it just from waking up. We continue the trend even as we sleep. I've been blessed to be around powerful manifestors. I didn't discount myself.

The biggest manifestation for me was making my health what it is today. It's been some years since I started the journey. I'm still in awe of what I accomplished.

As I got those points, I went, *"Hmm. I got it."* What did I get? What my Mind Over Matter Unlimited is.

When people think of resurrection, they think of life. I didn't just want weight loss. I wasn't only focused on diabetes reversal. I wanted a new life for myself. I yearned for a better connection with body, heart, mind, and soul.

I heard:

Welcome to Mind Over Matter Unlimited!

It is where health resurrection manifests. Life starts anew in the mind. What follows will awe you.

I took my mission statement to people I knew. They loved it. Agreed, that was completely what Zachary Shiloh Watts would say. It matches my energy with words.

Three people were really interested. I smile not only because writing in international best-selling books built me as a writer. I wound up manifesting a group of clients.

Geneva Hill has been one of my best friends. So has her husband, Justin. The Hills came to me because each wanted help with their respective health. They felt working with me would get them to where they wanted.

Paula Eberling came into my life in late 2021. She did so as *Magical Miracles* drew closer. As we got to know each other, she explained her medical history. Paula wanted to get her own health better (with someone with whom she had a real connection). Paula felt bonded to me by my BLK Lion's Roars, my podcast, and my overall being.

I took what I learned from my past coaching experiences. Added what I learned in building my general business. I laid out the tools for my success to all of them. I wanted to give the founding MOMU members better than what I had. They deserved it.

So, what makes Zachary Shiloh successful? What got me to this point? What do I offer my clients?

Partners In Believing

On October 28, 2019, I made a decision. I was three days away from seeing my doctor. I wanted to change my life for the better. I decided to get rid of social media.

Social media (at the time) was becoming too much for me. I already felt disconnected from some people across multiple platforms. The worst place was on Twitter. Didn't help that I knew I was depressed (plus taking Zoloft to battle this).

I was on social media less for over six months. If anyone contacted me, it was via email. Otherwise, I thought I was on my own. As of this book release, it's been over three years since that time.

I heard the term *"Partners in Believing"* when I was in the DreamBuilder program. I would listen to it under a different name. Like Mary Morrissey, Bob Proctor was influenced by Napoleon Hill. Napoleon Hill has no relation to Geneva and Justin Hill.

Napoleon Hill interviewed some of the richest people in our world. He would eventually write a book called *Think and Grow Rich*. I have read it. When I did, it was for Brave Thinking Masters.

Hill laid out there were thirteen rules to success. One of them was called The Mastermind. What is a Mastermind (or Partner in Believing)? It is someone (or individuals) who encourages you to go after whatcha want.

When I started Mind Over Matter Unlimited, I thought I had no one in my corner. I forgot that I had people in my life (as I began my health resurrection). As of September 3, 2022, I was utterly wrong. Memories of something useful I mentioned (very early in this book) flooded my mind. As a matter of fact, I wasn't aware of this because I was applying it subconsciously.

For the purpose of this book, it did begin with me leaving social media. A co-worker of mine named Cathy encouraged me to leave there (if it was gonna make me feel better). Unbeknownst to Cat, it was doing wonders for me.

I was becoming more alert. I was focused on my tasks. My personality was livelier. I took my daily breaks willingly. I let go of enduring with no real rest (outside of bathroom and lunch).

I opened up about my health to other people. One person was Raymond Gallagher. He was my surrogate dad for many years. Ray was a father figure to the woman I left (in 2019) as well. He loved his biological family, Pro Wrestling, Catholic faith, and general life.

He loved that I got rid of social media. I was happy that I would hang out with him (during the weekend). Saw my changes without it. He felt that I was more relaxed. Introduced me to people who came over to his house. He was comfortable enough to let me sleep over some nights (after I got my health in order).

I was happy and grateful to him. He lived long enough to see me beyond physical health. He was part of why I became a Catholic (for a bit). You saw how much I honored him in my chapter *Zachary Shiloh Blacks Out*.

I was fortunate to become a five-time best-selling author (while he was alive). I was with him at the launch of *Letters of Love II*. He jazzed out when I got my fourth best-seller. I'll never forget it.

The Coronavirus damaged our world. I knew my share of people who got the disease. Ray was one of them. He wound up passing away in January 2022. His sister, two children, and remaining biological family members continue living to this day.

Returning to Mind Over Matter Unlimited, I wanted there to be a support system. I yearned for people (who worked with me) to have others in their corner. To know they weren't alone as they put in effort (to better themselves).

I took what I learned from my friend/mentor, Jenn Morgan. I created an actual Mind Over Matter Unlimited Facebook group chat. I made it in spring 2022. When you read this, it will have been over six months since then.

We are our authentic selves. There is no sugarcoating in the chat. Uncensored language is encouraged. We stay politics-free. We bring problems that we face. We are a family.

Taking Chances, Making Mistakes, and Getting Messy

As Mind Over Matter Unlimited was turning half a year, I started rereading a particular book. It is over a year since I last did so. The work generally is forty-two days.

There is a morning reflection. A daily affirmation to be applied. An evening exercise finishes the day. I write out what is asked, plus more.

I was on my second day of this new run. I talked with a person or two (before an afternoon Zoom call). The topic was around comfortability. It made me think of someone else briefly.

I mentioned three of my clients for Mind Over Matter Unlimited here. There was a fourth. I got a bit careless. I didn't ask this woman if she was okay with being in my group chat. I just added her for the sake of giving her community.

What I wanted was for her to see how I interacted with others. Believed that she would open up. Envisioned that she would work with me in/out of group chat. We went nowhere. I ultimately got her out.

I saw that as a failure. I was used to three people doing extraordinary things. Losing physical weight. Building themselves emotionally. Building their relationships with me, each other, and more.

I wound up getting a new client. A woman who I have been friends with (over a year when you read this). I knew her nature. I was hoping she'd join the Mind Over Matter Unlimited chat, but that one failure popped into my mind.

I reflected on the failure. Was it really such? No, it wasn't. I saw my former client as an opportunity. She paved the way for me to understand people better.

One of my favorite TV shows was called *The Magic School Bus*. It became cooler when I found out that it was a book series. I believe I watched every season (except for the Netflix version). I know that I read every single book.

The teacher's name was Valerie Frizzle. She took her students on daily field trips (to learn about our world). One thing she used to say is what I called this section. She would say to her pupils, *"Take chances, make mistakes, and get messy."*

I did such with every person that gave me time as a coach. Didn't matter if I was on my own or with a business partner. I saw the potential of others. I did my best to bring them out.

When I saw the lesson before me, I told my new client. As we kept chatting, I had a *"Coming to Jesus"* moment. I saw how uncomfortable the unnamed woman was. She was put there by force. I didn't want history to repeat.

Jen was more than just my new client. She was my friend. I loved her thoroughly. This made me think of not just her. I saw people who would work with me in the future.

Some will be for going into the group chat. Some will want to work with me only. I tried to respect all of my clients. I decided to ask people if they were okay (with being in the Facebook messenger group).

I applied that immediately. We both agreed that she shouldn't go in the group chat. We had our first solo call the next day. We got stronger together since.

Cold Showers

My earliest memories go back to me being two years old. I could see myself trying to get out of my crib. I remember sucking on a pacifier. I recalled running around happily.

One thing that I cherished as I grew up was a warm shower. I eventually leveled up the heat. That baby would perk me up to start my day. I would take two showers a day (depending on my preference).

I was looking to change in 2019. I felt like someone who had cancer. Diabetes was something I wanted to be gone. Be out of my body. I believed that I could reverse it. I looked into different things.

One thing that just popped into my head was a cold shower. I heard about chemotherapy. How cancer patients would ice themselves (or something like it). I researched the benefits of cold showers.

I didn't just rely on one website. I wanted to find multiple means of doing this. I asked and then received what I was looking for. More than one site listed the following benefits of cold showers:

Boosts immunity

Relaxes sore muscles

Improves blood circulation

Helps deal with depression and anxiety

Makes skin better

Brings a sense of discipline

I was off from work on November 1, 2019. I didn't shower once. I remember the above. Decided to take a straight cold shower. It kinda bothered me a pinch, but I loved myself for doing it (when I got out).

Let's jazz this section a bit. Time to introduce another fandom. One I can say proudly that I am in is the James Bond community. Agent 007 was one of the coolest characters that I ever saw.

The dude had it all. He was well-trained in combat. He was a smart man beyond fighting. He drove numerous cars. He had diverse gadgets. He had sexy ladies.

All of that was nice to be, do, and have. There was one thing I learned that I didn't foresee. I had no clue that how James Bond showered would be something I apply (in my 30s). I didn't fathom that Agent 007 would be part of my health resurrection.

I learned that my preferred way to shower is called the "James Bond Shower." He'd start off warm (or hot) and then finish off with cold. Hearing this unknowingly would motivate me for years.

Inner Child

One thing people say that they love about me is how loving I am. Why is that so? I believe that I never grew up completely. I remained a child at heart.

I have reminders of my childhood. I still have action figures that I played with. They haven't been used by me in decades. They watch over me like guardian angels.

I loved being in nature. I talked in my chapter (for an unmentioned book) about how I enjoyed going to the park. If not there, then I would be fine with being in the backyard.

I repeatedly expressed how proud I am to be a geek. I was since being Little Zachary Shilohkins. I really enjoyed watching cartoons. I loved the stuff where I got seasons with characters.

They would inspire me. They encouraged physical activity. They let me know that it's alright to be smart. They would make me cry.

You have seen what my life has been like since 2019. I felt a significant disconnect from my inner child. I was beating myself up. Things that I loved weren't enjoyable. Didn't help that I was in tune with people who were more adult than me.

It sucked being around folks who were bleak about their futures. Their existence was mainly about money. They weren't treating themselves right. They rubbed off onto me.

I thought I was okay with "once in a while" beer. I gorged myself on food. I wasn't entirely optimistic. I was about not having fun anymore.

I couldn't feel my inner me. I was becoming more soulless as the days went by. I found out about my depression. It was a relief to know why I wasn't as warm.

I wasn't only about weight loss (as I repeatedly hammered in this book). I wasn't just for fixing my mind. I wanted to be light again. I was looking to move out where I was; however, I began reconnecting with myself there.

I began looking for stuff that made me laugh. I loved to chuckle a lot. I found a comedy special by Robin Harris. It was what inspired one of my favorite childhood films called *Be Be's Kids*.

I started listening to a podcast called *Unleash Your Inner Creative*. It is hosted by Lauren LoGrasso. It reminded me that I was a creative person. Been so since my childhood.

Lauren brought on some people for interviews. I found a common thread. She would ask, "If a little you stood in front of you, what would you say? What would he/she think?"

I thought about that (after I moved back in with my parents). My little me would be in awe of my present self. I'd tell him that what I went through was real.

I worked on my inner child for months. He automatically comforted me in the early Coronavirus pandemic days. I was at work. I had to tell numerous families of the nursing home residents that they couldn't see their loved ones physically. The closest thing to that is via video cam.

My little me was in my lap. He handed me my childhood plush named Mr. Puppy. We made the phone calls for the remainder of my day. I was crying a bit. Since then, he has been my best friend.

I can tell when he's around. I can hear his legit voice. I can feel him when my smile is hard. He checks on me when I hurt myself (by mistake).

Shadow Work

Life isn't all sunshine. Rainbows don't fill the skies heavily. There are days when it rains from sun up to dusk. To quote Peter Pan (from Hook), *"To live is quite an awfully big adventure."*

As I continued to work on this blessed venture, I went through my share of heartaches. I was reminded of the relationships I had. I was coming close to the three-year anniversary of when I got told of my depression. I was arriving nearer to when I began really cherishing (this meat bag called) my body on Halloween 2019.

My last real romantic relationship end date will never leave me. Again, it was officially on November 23, 2019. Writing this book forced me to open up wounds that I had to heal further. Recall even times that I thought were lost to me.

I believe my relationship actually ended on September 13, 2019. My then fiancée and I had our final overnight stay in Atlantic City. We stayed for two to three days.

I went to a press conference for a Mixed Martial Arts/Pro Wrestling event called Bloodsport. The actual show was the following evening. That would be a breeding ground for trouble ahead (I didn't foresee).

I recall us leaving to return to Staten Island. We had this programming of being upset as an evening (or more) would become a memory. I felt this thing of having to leave early. I knew that we'd have to face reality. I would have rather had got it over with than delay the inevitable.

Tragedies multiplied onto me.

The fighting with my ex-fiancée (who I have been without for three years in 2022) was daily. She wasn't happy with me completely. She brought up how I let her down. How our lives were absolute shit. Why didn't we make anything of ourselves?

Me?

I wasn't a hero. I was disgusted with her on my end. I had some spite towards her. One thing followed me for the better part of four years. That was her getting her driver's license on the first try.

An old habit of hers resurfacing without my knowing. If she told me, I got irate because she knew I didn't tolerate it. I tried my best to hide myself, but I couldn't really disguise my authentic self.

I knew my anger was intense. I didn't see it as a crutch. I saw it as something that could be positive. I would spend my remaining 2019 turning this into discipline.

One of my favorite Marvel Cinematic Universe scenes is from the *Marvel's Avengers* movie. It is towards the end. Captain America (played by Chris Evans) says to Dr. Bruce Banner (played by Mark Ruffalo), *"Now is a really good time for you to get angry."* Banner replies, *"You wanted to know my secret. I'm always angry."* After Banner gives his long-awaited answer, he becomes The Incredible Hulk and joins the team for the final battle.

I always remembered it. I applied that to myself. I am always angry. That is the truth.

We, human beings, are the same as animals. We are born at a specific time. We are growing up every single day. We change our outside skin. We all have emotions.

Anger is an emotion. It is like sadness, happiness, and gratitude. I didn't want to suppress my feelings. I wanted to live them out.

My clients asked me, *"What keeps you calm?"* I am the real me. I don't hold back.

I acknowledge that I am angry. I live it as an emotion. What else helps?

I accepted that I myself was a shadow. I was a reflection. I mirrored the world around me. I was attached to certain people. I was darkness itself.

I have experienced my share of threats throughout my life. One of my earliest memories was in Pre-K. I had speech therapy for my autism. A grown man threatened to call my parents if I didn't do what he wanted me to do. I mentioned this in my chapter for the overwhelm book (I didn't name).

This would trigger what is called "Fight or flight." I didn't know it back then. I just wanted to be a good kid. That moment programmed something else in me. As I aged, I came to find out that it would be called trauma.

Doing shadow work helps me confront my past. Allows me to exist in a stressful world presently. Brings me comfort as I walk into an unwritten future.

Whenever you read this, I have been with Amazon for over two years. I mentioned my career there through this book (without naming the retail jungle until *Magical Miracles*). I would love to share something for this section.

Many people don't know my name. I am recognized, though. This was shown to me as I worked through the summer of 2022.

A section of Amazon is called AFE. I am part of what they call Ship Dock. For some odd reason, there was a switch-off between the two for the Tote Stacker division. People knew me as the leader of that division.

Folks were in awe to see me doing something else. The main question I heard was, *"Why is the leader of the Tote Stackers here?"* Many thought that I was from AFE. That was never the case.

AFE wanted their people only (as of summer 2022). Me? I went to pull cages off trucks all day. I still do that up to four times a week (to make my living).

I built a reputation of not just leading the Tote Stacker division. I would bring some snacks every day. I did this from December 2021 through spring 2022. Folks would thank me for doing that. They would say that it showed I cared.

This is where shadow work benefitted me.

There was a Puerto Rican guy from AFE. He irked the living shit outta me. He did so on different levels. He showed me his true self. I saw it myself.

I would get the snacks at a specific point. I wanted to know if things were good in Tote Stacker. I would bring the stuff. The food was dibbed. The team (plus our general co-workers) would eat (during the day to stay nourished).

Unnamed noticed there were no snacks (at times). He went through three personality changes. He asked me if I could go get some. He would beg for me to go. The one that got me rallied up most was when he would demand me to get the shit.

I asked him to stop calmly. He kept going. It got to the point where I had enough. I learned from an incident involving two guys (over a year now).

The younger male kept sticking his nose in the elder's business. The elder literally violated the non-violence policy. Amazon doesn't condone shoving. To quote a Metallica song, *"Sad but true."*

Beggerkins violated my space. He wasn't my friend. He almost got a beatdown. Only one other person got on that level. That was Sabretooth.

I reminded myself of the non-violence violation. This hat wasn't worth it. His bitching, moaning, groaning, or _____ wasn't worth me losing my job.

I returned to work on May 16, 2022. I made it known to Beggerkins that I was not gonna be walked on by him (or anyone else). If I got snacks, then it was when I went. Not because he tells me to.

Can things get better? Yes. I put him on blast for the other workers to see, hear, and feel. From that day forward, he still talked his shit, but I put his ass in place.

One of my favorite Pro Wrestlers was named Taz. He had this phrase: *"I don't need a weapon. My hands are my weapons."* Beggerkins learned Zachary Shiloh's words are sharp as knives. Other people know that as well.

Intermittent Fasting/My Abundance

On October 31, 2019, I had clarity about my health. I was determined to fix my problems. I was browsing the internet for help. I searched for diabetes reversal.

Google would lead me to Dr. Jason Fung. Dr. Fung suggested this thing called Intermittent Fasting. You can eat within a specific timeframe. After that, you had to let your body relax.

Intermittent Fasting helped expose me to other things than what I saw.

I could see myself unemployed for x amount of time. I would not just binge-watch TV shows. I binged on food and non-water. It didn't help me that I was consuming heavy sugars. I thought for years that I was untouchable.

I would hold my heart a lot. I was out of breath. I almost fainted during an actual press conference (for work). I had memory problems so bad that I forgot my name was Zachary Shiloh Watts completely. I had struggled to fall asleep (especially at night).

It got worse when I got paid employment in the nursing home. I was near vending machines consistently. Candy. Gum. Soda.

The thing that nearly got me the most was green tea. What? Isn't that supposed to be very healthy? I didn't know throughout the years that companies (such as Arizona and

Nestle) had sugar in their products. There was extra sugar on top of what was there.

In BLK Lion's Roar, I believe I shared that I learned the shocking truth from a friend. I was at Tim Horton's (following grocery shopping on a Saturday morning). Donuts were my biggest foodie pleasure. I loved my breakfast sandwiches. All of that being washed down with tea, juice, or soda.

I would really listen from that conversation onward. I would take what was said to heart. I began reading labels more strongly. I believe my own body became an ally. It would react to certain foods or drinks.

I would cringe after channeling my Walking Nutritional Facts mode. If not shake, then remind myself of why I was at this point. I noticed that other people seemed to be miserable. How I wanted to be a better human being.

It wasn't an overnight success. I kept pushing myself. I loved my bullshit. I didn't think I could live without all that made me sick. I never thought that I would go without these items.

As I started to keep that main idea in my head, the world began to change around me. I remembered what year it was. 2019 was still the year. I wasn't just near being with my now ex for a decade. I was reaching a much-needed repeat.

I saw myself in 2009. I was a vegetarian. I stopped eating candy. I didn't consume fast food heavily. I wasn't drinking tea, juice, or soda. I wasn't having anything with sugar (except what fruit and cereal I loved at the time).

Before I met the woman I went to love for over nine years, I lost tremendous weight. I was happier. I was slimmer. I was heavily active.

The most significant difference was me being a meat eater (in 2019). I had stronger protein than I did prior. I was humbled by what I produced. I believe I cried tears of joy. I still do (as I continue to celebrate my success).

We, human beings, love to harp on the negative. I mentioned a certain Beggerkins from my day-to-day job. You saw the result of him thinking his rude ass would abuse me.

I was off from work on September 17, 2022. I was thinking about the blessings of Intermittent Fasting. I just began doing a fast for a full day. It made me think of the homeless (or houseless, as George Carlin would call them).

It hurts me knowing folks (across the world) go without. It is a huge blow to watch a person have to ask (or beg) for a dollar. It sucks when you know folks are sleeping on the street. It cuts when you know that many aren't eating daily.

Intermittent Fasting puts a greater appreciation of my life (in perspective). I had my share of surgeries as a child. I have been an adult for eighteen years. I am blessed to say that I haven't had any surgeries in my adulthood.

I have had my share of injuries in that time. The good news is I was able to nurse myself. I took whatever medication. I made massive changes I had to.

What is abundance? If I ask you what abundance is, I can hear the possibilities. Some will think having unlimited money.

A thought in mind is a flashy house. An idea would be driving numerous cars. Another picture is a non-biological family member cleaning where ya live, cooking meals, and resolving other domestic stuff.

In the biography I used for my co-authoring books, I have stated that I am an all-life New Yorker. I was born here in Winter 1987. My birthplace is Brooklyn. For the last twenty-six years of my life, I have resided in Staten Island.

If someone were to come see Zachary Shiloh, they would be in awe of where he lives. They take a look at the exterior then they'd probably say, *"Holy shit. I can't believe he lives there. He's gotta be rich."*

This makes me think of myself growing up. People have called me Carlton Banks. They have done so by how I present myself. I have a high vocabulary. I dressed in polo shirts, khaki pants, and other corporate-looking attire. Kept myself groomed for the most part.

What is abundance?

I used to believe the answers that I stated. I can thank TV shows such as *Fresh Prince of Bel Air*. I think it was glorified in music videos. We read about individuals (real or imagined) such as Richie Rich, Donald Trump, and much more.

There is a gross misinterpretation of what abundance is. It didn't take me living until "old age" to see the light. Age is nothing but a number. I experienced this before I even hit the age of thirty-six.

The house where my family resides is not my home. One of the greatest Luthor Vandross songs is called *"A House is Not A Home."* A house is just a building. It's the same as a church, library, and store.

Home is where my heart is. It lives multidimensionally as you've read. It's with other people. It's in my podcast. It lies in my co-authorings.

Abundance is living another day. Wealth is applying my senses daily. I'm fortunate to eat and drink without tubes.

I mentioned that others called me Carlton Banks. Tom Jones wasn't my favorite singer. I wasn't in nobody's glee club. I wasn't valedictorian of any graduating class I was in.

I never attended a prep school. I got into physical fights as I aged because other guys thought I was weak. I knew what racism was before I reached adulthood.

The largest difference between Carlton Banks and me is I spent a good wad of my teenage years looking for work. I understood my parents' blood, sweat, and tears were from their hard work (since I was little). Their sacrifices led to them being homeowners, having cars, going away for days (without their three children), etc. I didn't yearn to sponge off them.

My efforts did pay off. I wound up being employed more than once. I made my own money.

What got me all of my jobs?

My ability to communicate. Having people in my life growing up (with no ties to the Watts family). How I presented myself through the years. My interactions with employed staff. Also, I have the ability to adapt to my surroundings and then apply my knowledge.

Speaking of my family, what makes me prosperous is knowing I exceeded them (in different ways). No member of my family has a podcast. None of them were featured in international best-selling books. The older members can't say they reversed diabetes. None can say they had their own business (in their thirties).

The most remarkable piece of abundance I can say is I am happy and grateful. For? The air I breathe. The food that I eat. The liquids I drink. The roof over my head. The money in my wallet.

For opportunities to write books like this. To see myself grow every day. To know people around this beautiful Earth.

Exercise

Weight Training

I loved going outside as a kid. As I got older, I started to admire people with bodies better than my own (or so I thought). I really adored the "bodybuilders" I saw.

I would go to gyms throughout the years. I recall the earliest was me being twelve years old. I went to the gym with my dad at the YMCA. I don't know why we stopped going (besides money issues). We'd try again after I was an adult. It didn't bear any fruit because of the same result.

I would try again on my own. No real success. It discouraged me to stop.

I would have one last try. It was three to four years before my diagnosis in 2019. My partner couldn't handle the stress on their body and wound up ending their membership to our local Crunch gym.

In BLK Lion's Roar, I believe I said that I returned to the New York Manhattan Hotel in late 2019. The oddly nicknamed NYMA had a gym. I was determined to lose my weight. I wanted to reverse my diabetes. I didn't just want to be in my room.

I would go to the NYMA gym. I used their weight equipment. I was stunned at what I did. I recalled being able to lift their max-level weight. This would cause me to return twice more (before I had to checkout).

I see why I looked better (when I returned to Staten Island). Felt as such to other people. I was physically active. I did something I hadn't done in years to that point. I had no reason to be shamed.

I explained what the Coronavirus Pandemic has done to our world. I'm sure you have your own description. No need to compare notes. We can all agree that the results are mainly negative.

I'm happy and grateful for the bad. Why? There was some good from it for me. Let's get to how.

The Coronavirus, as I said, shut down businesses. Some to say were gyms, unfortunately. People around the world weren't able to get their means of physical activity. It would be months to years before they got to do such.

Me? I was fortunate that I bought my own dumbbell weight set in December 2019. I didn't want to waste money on a gym membership. It came from the history I laid out in this section.

I wanted to exceed what I could do at the NYMA. I went to amazon.com and then made my purchase. When I got it, I awed myself on the same day. I carried that heavy thing (from out of where I lived) to my room. I would use that exact set (on and off) the whole pandemic. I still continue to do so as you are reading this.

Boxing/Sparing

I loved the Rocky movie series. The most recent (as I am writing this book) is *Creed II*. I loved watching the training stuff. It showed how the characters better conditioned themselves.

When I started with my health resurrection, I began watching Creed again. It motivated me to shadowbox. I'm not fighting any human being. I'm sparing with myself.

I would do it practically every day. I never stopped. I thought of my medical issues. I saw them as my biggest adversaries. I trained myself to face them head-on.

I wound up purchasing Mixed Martial Arts gloves. They looked like regular boxing gloves. They did several things for me.

My hands were protected as I worked out. I felt like a professional fighter. I got quicker in their removal. My general reflexes improved over time.

Martial Arts Weapon Use

I have been a Martial Arts fan since I was little. I mentioned that Berry Gordy's *The Last Dragon* was an influential movie in my life. I loved the self-defense by Leroy. I thought it was cool to see him fight armed thugs with his own weaponry. It would be the genesis of other martial arts-related media in my life.

What else did I watch? I mentioned *Highlander* in *Ascension Visionary Leaders*. It wasn't just known for the quickening (or reincarnation point). I loved the sword battles.

Another influence was the Teenage Mutant Ninja Turtles. I loved these four turtles (who were named after real-life Renaissance artists). My favorite was Raphael. He was the badass of the group.

2022 had been quite a year. I wanted to add something to my workout routine. Something that could give me more discipline.

I bought a sword and ninja Sais (or daggers) in June 2022. The sword eventually was trashed because it broke. What a shame? That's okay because I still have the Sais.

I bought a bow staff in October 2022. I would have nunchucks in November 2022. These things had built my overall discipline.

Jump Rope

When I was a lad, I used to see girls (like my sister) use these ropes to jump around in. I was invited to partake in the activity. I wasn't good at it. I got discouraged and then stopped bothering. This is partly why I became a couch potato.

Remember when I mentioned my final time in Atlantic City? It wasn't memorable only for what I stated. I could see myself waking before sunrise. I left my fiancée as she slept every morning. I would go outside to take in the morning air.

I would jump rope. I wasn't perfect with it. I did my few jumps, then walked until I was ready to return to my woman. I kept the trend going until winter. I don't know what happened, but two plus years passed.

I felt an urge in September 2022. I mentioned the Rocky film series' influence on me. I was watching Adonis Creed train for his final fight in *Creed*. He is seen jumping rope in a gym. This would cause me to remember Rocky's training.

Rocky would jump rope to prepare for his final fights. I watched these trainings repeatedly as September 2022 was closing. They would motivate me to do it every day. I was determined. I wasn't looking for five to ten repetitions (when I bought my new rope). I was fine with just two.

It didn't matter if I was indoors or outdoors. I was gonna jump rope. I could feel my confidence grow. It was something I could do as a pre-work warm-up.

Juggling

I loved the circus since I was a child. One of my favorite parts was watching the clowns. They were throwing things in circular motions. This would follow me like a jump rope.

As I headed into my second week of jump roping in 2022, I would add this to my regimen. I understand why I loved watching the clowns even more. They got to be silly. They did their routine to music as well.

I found this to be relaxing. I got quicker with it. I built another excellent habit. I found increasing humor. I started whistling more.

It became something I could do at work (in the last five minutes of mealtimes). It would give me a positive time user. I got my thoughts together. It helped me overcome sickness.

Pull-ups

When I was a lad, I admired guys who were older than me. I would see them at parks I loved. One was Jackie Robinson Park. Jackie Robinson Park was the park by Community School 21. Community School 21 was where I went to school (from third grade through sixth grade).

Community School 21 has more meaning for me. My father and his siblings went there as children. My little sister was there from Pre-K through fifth.

The older males would pull themselves off the ground. They did so off monkey bars. I felt like I was watching a stronger version of the circus. I thought only circus performers did amazing feats like that. I was happily wrong.

I tried to be like them as a child. It didn't work out for me. I see why. Like other things in my life, I got discouraged by it. What do you do when you are defeated?

You give up. You run away. You let that dream die. You hope to let this become something you forgot.

Many years would pass by. I keep bringing up things (in this book). Not to live a loved Prince song (called *Joy of Repetition*), but I see how they helped shape me into the man I am today.

Pull-ups would come back into my life as I was reaching my thirties. It would return to me in multidimensional ways. This would mainly be from comic book lure.

I am a huge Batman fan. When I became employed in my longest job, I saw *Batman vs Superman* in theaters with my girlfriend. I will never forget one of the most incredible scenes.

I was always a fan of how Batman conditioned himself. How dedicated he was to honing his body. We see him do that in the 2016 movie release. Bruce Wayne (outside of the Batman suit) is seen training. He was so badass.

Bruce was weight training with dumbbells. He used a sledgehammer on a tire. Bruce pulled a tire up to the fire. The thing that I recall the most was him doing pull-ups (with weights on him). As the now-confirmed minute montage ends, he lets out primal groans, moans, yells, or _____.

A Batman-like character has been on the CW TV network for about two seasons. That is the Green Arrow. The television series was simply called *Arrow*.

I recall one of my greatest podcasting influences talking about *Arrow* weekly. For the love of that show, I'm surprised there weren't actual reviews of that by people. They claimed that *Arrow* season one was better in writing than *World Wrestling Entertainment* (which they watched and then reviewed every week).

I was kinda skeptical about it. I didn't just hear these two plus-sized guys. I heard other people (who had no ties) talk about the comic book archer. I said, *"Okay. Why not?"*

I made time to watch. I wound up seeing the first *Arrow* season in full. When I was done, it was just as *Arrow* season two was getting ready to premiere.

What I loved about *Arrow* was the training by Oliver Queen (played by Stephen Amell). He wasn't just sparing with his "bodyguard" named John Diggle (played by David Ramsey). He did actual pull-ups. His way was more shocking to me.

Oliver would do his pull-ups from one point and then go higher. He'd stop for a bit. He reversed himself until he got down. The most remarkable thing regarding this is that there was no stunt double. Stephen Amell himself did these training montages.

The last influence returns as a movie series I touched upon. That is *Rocky.* As I rewatched these scenes, I saw Rocky and Adonis Creed, respectively, pulling themselves off the ground. Something clicked within me. I felt the pull.

I decided to go for it. I began doing this again in May 2022. I kept the images in my mind. I could hear Rocky coaching Adonis in their pieces of training. I felt like Batman. I was focused like Arrow.

I tested myself. I found out I could pull myself off park poles. I could do it off street lights. I did this initially about twice a week. I felt my confidence build, then decided to do it three to seven times a week.

Meditation

It is something that many watch on TV. It's something utilized in random movies. A topic discussed in other books.

Meditation is a clearing of the mind. It is the focusing of a person's energy positively. It is an expression of one's higher self. Another word to use is channeling.

In 2019, I was looking for a therapist (or someone) to talk with about my problems. What I was really looking for was something a bit deeper. A connection that wasn't on a time limit. A means of channeling morning, afternoon, or evening. Something I could use anywhere (regardless of work, where I live, etc.).

When I found meditation (or, more so, reunited with it), I thought of the most common way. I found that it is multi-dimensional. There are different forms of this.

Music

According to my mother, this has been in my life since I was in her womb. My father would play some of his favorite stuff. It would only grow more as I did.

I heard it everywhere. I had it in school. It was in stores I went to. It was in restaurants I ordered from (or ate at). It was at social events (such as parties, conventions, and Pro Wrestling shows).

I learned the power of this as I was writing this section. Music was comforting for me. It calmed me down when I was most angry. I laughed at some lyrics. I was bonded to the singer, band, writer, and producer.

Journaling

As I have witnessed my life since childhood, journaling has been part of it. Some of the most memorable TV characters weren't fighting foes with martial arts. They didn't drink themselves with alcohol. They weren't adults.

They were kids at the same time. If they were older, then they were teenagers. They were the narrators of their own shows (or character-centric episodes). Some of my favorite characters were Doogie Howser, M.D., Doug Funnie, and Sue Ellen Armstrong.

The above were very creative souls. They were articulate when in discussions. They seemed to be active for their ages.

I wanted to be just like them. I wouldn't find my fire until later in life. I'm not beating myself up by any means. I love this very much.

When I was diabetic, this was the first thing I saw as I laid out. I did recall the TV characters I named (at the time). I saw what journaling did for them.

It didn't judge them. They were their own best friend. Gave them the chance to recap the ending day. It was a pre-bedtime stress reliever. Allowing them to make their most authentic feelings known.

I received all I stated. I was blessed with more. I have a written archive. I can relive specific days. I can go back in time to console my younger self (for things he didn't manifest).

Standing still

One of the greatest video games in history is called Street Fighter. It has been around for over thirty years. When I was a kid, there were two movies. One was a live-action film starring Jean Claude van Damme. The other motion picture was in what Japanese animation fans called Anime.

There were two cartoon series. The first was from the early 1990s. The other was based off the Anime movie. The Anime series called *Street Fighter IIV* was more memorable for me. Why?

It would unknowingly play a role in my getting my health together. I remember the Ryu character traveling around Earth with his best friend, Ken. The two eventually end up in India. They would meet a wise sage named Dhalism.

Dhalism helped unlock what is known as Hado. Hado can be translated as universal energy. Another way to say it would be Reiki. Ryu got his awakened quicker than Ken.

To help him start channeling his newfound power, he stands still for a bit. Ryu would make circular motions with his arms.

He would feel the ki come to his hands and then blast it in physical form. As I witnessed it, I could sense there was peace within Ryu.

I would do that pose on and off throughout my adulthood. It came better when I wanted to improve myself through meditation. It would bring me to another version I could do standing up.

I learned of the chakras. These energy points while watching *Street Fighter IIV*. They reappeared in my life before my second fiancée arrived. I wouldn't work with them again for over a decade.

They have reignited when I was under the guidance of a gay couple. I would eventually leave them over circumstances. I later found my now 2X co-author in Geneva Hill.

Gen was doing a course in the fifth dimension. It was there that she did this pose, standing up. It allowed her to be grounded by utilizing the heart chakra. I would practice it for several days. The heart chakra pose brought me comfort.

I wound up applying it when I take a cold shower. It helped me get centered as I felt the cold water splash my body. I felt like a monk while doing so.

Sitting down

This is the most known form of meditation for many. It was the one I used most myself. I wanted to be able to deal with people. I had nasty anxiety. I wanted to exist.

I researched meditation. Watching other people do or talk about this, I remembered shows like *Kung Fu: The Saga Continues* and *Vanishing Son*. The main characters utilized martial arts but weren't always in battle. They were seen with their legs crossed, hands together, and eyes closed.

This allowed them to focus their energy inward. It helped their physical bodies to heal. Brought forth clarity to their thoughts. As a kid, I thought that was cool.

For me? I experienced that, plus more. The legendary Abraham Hicks came into my life circa 2020. It was during the Hay House 2020 *You Can Heal Your Life Summit*.

As I watched more of Abraham, I learned more about manifestation. He did attribute the Law of Attraction. One thing I got was we are always manifesting. All it takes is just seventeen seconds.

I had no clue that this would lead me to a life I didn't see. A more substantial structure for stuff I was doing. Bring forth knowledge I thought was useless because of failures (which were really successes).

Martial arts weapon use

Martial Arts weapons aren't just a means of self-defense (or physical activity). They have aided me in some of my most stressful times in 2022. It doesn't take me long.

Just two minutes of use is enough. As I used them, whatever was stressing me would subside. I found that I was able to think of positive things. I witnessed myself getting aligned with the goals I sought. I bonded with some people spiritually.

I was able to breathe stronger. I went at a slower pace. I could sense energy more.

Podcasting

The Flowtastic Zone where love shines brightest. Home of the BLK Lion's Domain. The place where Zachary Shiloh roamed around the Earth. Allowed for multigenerational people to partake in what I call Universal Grounding.

My podcast is called *BLK Lion's Airspace*. I wasn't just talking to a person by myself. I had spoken to other males. I chatted with sensational females.

Before there ever was a BLK Lion's Domain, it was all just me talking. I had a multi-dimensional means of doing so. I did it off my desktop. I vocalized on my mobile devices.

I am one hundred percent me. I don't have to sugarcoat anything. I'll be pissed off. I will cry like a baby. I laugh so hard that my face hurts.

I was already in a form of therapy for months in 2019. As I look back, I don't just see my podcast as a means of meditation for me. Every single podcast guest appearance I did. I've been channeling myself for over four years now.

I see myself. What you get in my podcast is exactly how I was off before my pilot episode. I never let up after my show was born.

I talked to the hosts about whatever we chatted about. Frustrations with what we were together for. The joy of the said product for the minutes to hours heard, viewed, or written.

Whatever amount of time was for us. These moments stayed in my heart. I cherish them every day.

Cooking

When I was physically little Zachary Shiloh, I loved watching people cook. I never memorized recipes (except seldom ones). I just loved how peaceful they looked. I wanted that serenity for myself.

My grandmothers died four to five years apart. Their deaths (or homecomings) occurred in my late twenties to early thirties. How do I know? They respectively passed in my birth month of January.

I recalled being around them. My dad's mom was more around because I lived with her until after my tenth birthday. Ma Watts was the one who made me pancakes. I had homemade pasta with sauce. She was the first person I knew who made cookies, cakes, and other pastries.

Nana Kitchings was the one who showed me what "Soul Food" was. I knew it before there was a movie (by that exact title). Our family always had some style of chicken, collard greens, cornbread, and more.

Each woman never complained about politics. Didn't try to goad me into doing things with black history. There was one thing only. Love for the general human race.

I would find my way through cooking as I grew up. I initially boiled water for hot dogs. I would make pasta, veggies, and other meat. I didn't really notice this as a meditation. I was living to honor a friend (who saved my life).

It didn't dawn on me until this book was in production. I took a break from writing, and then it came to me as I was in nature. Not just that, but I thought of the woman I spoke of most (not named Blair Hayse). She was my second fiancée.

I remembered how she was. Part of her strength was in the kitchen. She loved being there. I was sad during our relationship because she'd make things with cheese. It sucked for me as a lactose intolerant.

That made me cry at times. I thought I was a hindrance to her. I asked, *"How could a person like her love a person such as me? Wouldn't she want someone who could enjoy all of her cooking?"*

As you read, that blessed soul put up with me for many years. She had me join her in stuff that we both could have. My love of cooking built up because of her. We had more homemade meals together than we ordered (or bought) takeout.

I noticed how happy we were. How we made our lives together (over time). When the food was done, we always ate somewhere in the house. May it be in her room, the kitchen, or the living room (for Thanksgiving or Christmas).

I came to cherish this, especially during the Coronavirus Pandemic. I saved hundreds of dollars I could have used on fast food. It gave me pure focus. I built a love for my own creations. I learned what I could or couldn't stand when I ate.

Cooking taught me not just my own sensitivities. I was reminded that I lived with four other people. I had to adapt to waiting until 7 AM to cook. This allowed my family to sleep without disturbance. Saved two family members from bothering me (about how I shouldn't cook between 3 AM and 7 AM).

Staying Consistent

Mel Robbins is one of the known people on Earth. I first discovered her in 2020. I was nearly a year into my health resurrection. I found Mel ala Hay House. Hay House was the company founded by Louise Hay (who was a legendary self-help teacher).

Hay House held its yearly *You Can Heal Your Life* event. Mel was one of the speakers. She spoke of something called a "Millionaire morning routine."

She talked about what made her successful. It was an impressive presentation. I remember it because the talk was one that I watched numerous times. Recalling her routine made me want to share some of mine.

Making up my bed

It is something many would say is a chore. Labeled by numerous folks as boring. Said to be a waste of time.

I didn't like doing this quite so much as a kid. Felt the same way through my 20s. I cherish this in my 30s.

It helps me organize my room. Allows me to get used to being on my feet for the day. Gives me an accomplishment to kick off my day. Doesn't have to be done perfectly.

My discipline built over time. I saw it as a form of exercise. It brought clearing of the mind.

Writing

I don't do this with pen to paper every day. I do it in my mind. I use the notes on my phone. I use Microsoft Word on a desktop or laptop.

Allows me to unload my thoughts. Paves the way for new ideas to come through. Manifest a better life, not just for myself.

Being in silence

We are surrounded by noise. Another word for noise is sound. Countless people start off their day with the news. Others go to the radio.

For many years of my life, I fit that mold of a person. I was blessed to be in the know with our world. I would pick up on things as I grew up.

As I said, we love being around negativity. Someone is dead from a mass shooting or suicide. Some Politician "took away" a liberty (or right). Climate Change is killing the human race.

I lived in places where television is utilized every hour of the day. If not, then the majority of the day by others. As the Coronavirus Pandemic grew, I sought to build my peace. I knew there were 24 hours in a day.

I loved times when no one I lived with was in the house. I didn't have to hear anything bad. If I wanted to nap, I could do as I please. If I wanted to cook, then I had no disturbances. Whatever I yearned for was mine to do, be, or have.

Sadly, the Coronavirus didn't only kill numerous people. It didn't just cripple businesses. I never had where I live entirely to myself (during this pandemic). I have seen my immediate family members practically all day, every day.

I heard people complain about different things. Some ramble on about not being able to do what they want (in a day). Not getting enough sleep is another. Not doing their own writings, podcasts, etc.

This brought me to cherish what time I do have even more. When I wake up for the day, I make it a mission to not have any audio on. Not my music. Not any motivational stuff.

I take it in that I have time where no one is up (besides me). I find that being in silence does help me. I get my clothes ready for the day. I update my writing logs. I meditate. I show appreciation that I am still alive.

Being Truthful

In this life, we all yearn to be loved. The feeling started in our adolescence. It manifested as we continued to age. Some actions were genuinely based on that desire. Other ways were from unseen negativity.

I discussed doing shadow work. How it helped me turn my anger into power. The same power allowed me to take charge of my life (especially in my workplace). I am happy and grateful for that.

I have tried my absolute best to be a good person. Some people understood me perfectly. Others didn't quite so well. I don't beat up myself for whomever has their perception.

As I thought about what really made me successful, I recall the relationships that I ended in my over three-year health resurrection. One saying that never left me is, *"The truth shall set you free."* Being truthful is one thing that makes me alive.

No one likes to be told, *"You suck."* When we receive negative feedback, our nervous system shuts down. A significant portion of us don't know how to handle it. We go into *"_____ didn't mean that. I'm a good person. I do only what is right for them."*

We'll go to other people who see us positively. They'll tell us what we want. That sends our brains the feel-good chemical called dopamine. We go about life like *"You suck"* never occurred.

Hearing *"You suck"* wasn't bad for me. I looked at myself. I thought, *"Okay, how do I improve?"* This came especially well as my previous romance was ending. My fiancée didn't flat out tell me I suck. I got the hint.

From that point forward, it was me being completely honest. People would ask me for my opinion on some things. If I loved whatever, I said go for it. If I disagreed, I would express such to the said person.

Being truthful has built confidence in myself. I do have an opinion. I am not voiceless.

Remember when I said that a certain Beggerkins learned the power of my words? How did other people get the hint as well? You can thank being truthful.

Knowing My Worth

As Mind Over Matter Unlimited was turning six months old, I was reaching a pinnacle. I didn't have clients for months at a time. I was fortunate to sniff one for a few weeks to a month. That's the truth.

I already knew what it was to be successful on an unpaid scale. I was seeing my clients grow. All of them were successful in business. They were making money on what they loved to do. They did so on a daily to weekly basis.

As I watched them, I asked myself, *"Why not me? How much longer can I do this unpaid?"* This would increase as evolution continued to build. This would manifest in my heart. This would bring out energy from my soul to my reality.

I was talking to random people I knew. Some were not members of Mind Over Matter Unlimited. I wanted to be paid for my services. Knew that I didn't just want to work my current (or any) day-to-day job forever. I was meant for more.

So, I'm asking about pricing. I heard some say that what I am doing is worth $350. They said it suits me because of who I am, what I am, and more.

As I looked into ways to help me get currency, I was gifted two means. I was already aware of them from paying for my co-authorings, tarots, and _____. One way was PayPal. The other was Venmo.

The actual price of working with me came as I thought about my general coaching journey. How I was approaching the actual birth of Mind Over Matter Unlimited. The accurate date is December 18, 2020.

As I laid out, it was initially called Love's Roar. It came as I worked with the most significant influence of Blair Hayse. That woman is Crystal Anne Davis.

I could hear Crystal in my head. I was off from work on September 30, 2022. It was by 6 AM EST. I was out of bed going into my second hour.

This would cement a price for me (or so I thought). It would give me a map for my forthcoming year. Not let me waver by any means.

I wanted $111 per person. I planned to move, but not quite how Crystal would. I would do the reverse. I was pretty new to asking for money to do what I loved. This made me think of other people.

What did I want more? Money or people? Money comes and then goes. I value having my own currency. I do, but I cherish human beings more (when I think of my general life adventure).

I thought, *"How can I get Huns to join me?"* I recalled my own struggles with money. How I scrapped to pay my bills. How I had to save shit tons to make a night away (from where I lived) happen.

This made me remember all of my best-selling authorships. How I just celebrated over two years since I joined Blairkins in *They Are Magic*. How I was scared of getting out the original *BLK Lion's Roar*.

Mind Over Matter Unlimited was six months old on October 28, 2022. I was gonna launch the paid version on that date. I wanted to start at $11.10. I planned to increase my price by another $11.10 every Friday until December 30th.

December 30th wasn't just the second to last day of the year. It held a bigger space in my heart. It was exactly a month before my birthday.

I'm not charging only because I want to get paid. I can speak as a decade old customer. I have bought my share of items through the years. I made use of things I did buy.

When there is a price tag to something, it adds more stakes for people. This burns more when it comes to health. People will stop at nothing to get their medicine, be seen by their doctor, or do whatever they gotta do. Why not pay for me?

Not Giving Up

After Mind Over Matter Unlimited turned six months exactly, I didn't receive any clients right away. I was posting on Facebook nearly every day. I was getting nothing (the majority of the time). I was being reminded of why I left social media (to some degree). I was somewhat contemplating (to leave the digital world again).

I would see other people (including my own clients) get reacted to. I was questioning myself. Would I get new people? Will I ever be paid for what I love?

I recalled my history since December 18, 2020. There were times when I didn't even sniff a person. I kept pushing on. I wouldn't tag anyone. I wasn't promoting books. I am not talking about myself (in general).

I'd talk about Love's Roar. How passionate I was. About how I wanted to be a Holistic Health Coach. My vision was to help people with their well-being in multidimensional ways.

As I recounted that, I could hear, *"One man can make a difference. And you are going to be that man."* That was the most powerful thing from *Knight Rider*. It made me think of the people involved in that show (such as David Hasselhoff, William McDaniel, and Patricia McPherson).

I could hear my own voice say, *"Not many people thought a dead police officer (with a talking car) was gonna be a hit TV show."* I gotta believe there was some doubt in the minds of show personalities. They were shockingly wrong.

Knight Rider lasted for four seasons. It spurned two television movies. The first was *Knight Rider 2000*. The other was *Knight Rider 2010*.

There were two other *Knight Rider* TV shows. *Team Knight Rider* from 1997 to 1998. *Knight Rider* from 2008 to 2009 (based on another TV movie).

The theme song itself (to my knowledge) was in three big songs. The first *Clock Strikes* by Timbaland and Magoo was released on April 14, 1998. Next was *Fire It Up* by Busta Rhymes (exactly a week later). *Beware of The Boys* by Punjabi MC in 2003.

There were two PlayStation 2 video games.

I could see something that exceeded *Knight Rider*... That is *Power Rangers*. It is soon to be 30 years old (when this book is read).

It premiered on August 28, 1993. I have seen every series. I owned all of the franchise movies. I played video games on Nintendo Game Boy, Sega Game Gear, Sega Genesis, and Super Nintendo. I watched the Radio City Music Hall on-stage event.

Read the different comic books (from Marvel to Boom Studios). Had posters on my bedroom wall (as a child). Played with varying figures of action.

I was at conventions where TV actors were. I was blessed to meet personalities from Boom Studios. I attended panels live from 2018 to 2020. I viewed virtual panels from Hasbro (since the Coronavirus pandemic began). I have listened to numerous *Power Rangers* podcasts.

Some of the most hardcore fans thought the franchise would have been dead by now. They were wrong. The podcasts are still being listened to. The TV shows transitioned from syndicated TV to cable TV to Netflix. The Boom Studios comic series is turning seven years old.

I have potential. Always did. I knew what I lost. I never forgot.

This is part of how I got the *BLK Lion's Airspace* name. I saw myself like Keith from *Voltron Legendary Defender*. He is a young hothead with love, commitment, and his own sense of patience. I saw myself becoming a leader like him.

I did become him somewhat. I kept this in mind as I forged my way with Mind Over Matter Unlimited. Believed that I would be seen. That I will attract what I sought. That whoever looked for me would come when the time was right.

How would this come together? By staying with social media. Continuing to do posts about not just Mind Over Matter Unlimited. Letting people see the real me.

Blessing What I Do Have / Not Giving Up Part II

Doing this book has allowed me to share my most precious memories. I cherished every single moment I had put into this. This is a culmination of hard work. So is Mind Over Matter Unlimited.

2022 saw me not just rebirth a business. Not only stay the course that I built for over two years. I confronted issues that have blocked me for years. We, human beings, have what are called limiting beliefs. They keep us in what we've been comfortable with.

This is what kept me small. It caused me not to do what I really loved before 2019. I let fears, insecurities, and intentions of others hold me back. I only carried my dreams in my mind. I couldn't execute them for what could go wrong. If it did not go right, then what I did lack?

Tell me if these are familiar....

"Why don't you go back to college?"

"You're wasting your time."

"What you do is bullshit."

"You need to face reality."

I recall how I reacted to these. I became stressed out. I would be sick for days at a time. I couldn't sleep. I didn't even bother trying to do anything. I let others paint me.

There were times when I did override the naysayers. What is a great example? I asked myself, *"If I wanted to be part of WrestleMania 35 weekend in 2019, what could I do? What do I have?"*

It started with the desire to go. It simply grew. I was led to different things.

I was employed by a nursing home. What did that provide for me?

I was knowledgeable about my scheduling. I didn't work every single day of the week. I was on the docket from Monday through Thursday. I accumulated time off.

Gave me a pain in the ass that I wanted to get away from. To break from the norm. To get out of my comfort zone.

I was making an income. My rent was met monthly over two years. Gas was put in the car that my woman drove. A symbol of providing for myself.

Money could help me pay for tickets to shows. I could purchase a hotel room to stay in (with my woman). I can buy merch (if we wanted that). I can get food and drinks throughout the said days.

I visualized myself having fun. I hear the enjoyment of other people. I felt the excitement rise as I got closer. I smelled the aromas that filled the air. I drooled from the taste of food, drinks, and whatever I partaken in.

I capitalized on ideas. I was able to do all of the above. Did so for four days and three nights.

After I ended the previous sentence, I paused for a bit. I blessed what I did. I could see where I was gonna go with Mind Over Matter Unlimited even more.

It is not about what I don't have. Living the present in happiness and gratitude. Preparing to receive a gradual increase.

I still had my non-paying clients. I had two paying clients. I continued building myself as my number one client.

GSD (Getting Shit Done)

One of the greatest Pro Wrestlers is The Rock. I geeked out about a fantastic feat that we shared. I still celebrate it every single day. No one can take that away from me. No employer, government, or other human being.

Many Pro Wrestling fans say his greatest rival was Stone Cold Steve Austin. I remember talking to childhood friends about it in sixth grade. I would make new friends in Junior High and then through High School. It continued into the present day in my workplace (and beyond).

Austin manifested a life that people (across the world) wanted to live. Dude was able to drive his pickup truck (into arenas). Caused what seemed to be millions of dollars in damages legally. He drank beer (while on the job). The best thing was beating the Hell out of his boss daily.

Stone Cold won his first World Title in 1998. The then World Wrestling Federation released a 60-minute video called *Austin 3:16 Uncensored*. The World Wrestling Federation Champion is told he has many remarkable traits. One happened to be his walk.

Then WWF lead announcer Jim Ross (better known as JR) asks him about it. The Texas Rattlesnake is downright blunt. This is the favorite part of Zachary Shiloh. I watched it many times. What does Stone Cold say?

With his theme song playing in the background, The Texas Rattlesnake classifies his walk as BMF. BMF is Bad Mother Fucker. His walk is a signal. That signal is Austin means business. When The Toughest Son of a Bitch in the WWF does his BMF, Stone Cold is ready to go. The WWF Champion is coming to beat another man's ass.

Stone Cold acknowledged people (such as JR) being in awe of him. Wondering how he does what he does. Also, how some guys get scared. That imprinted me for years.

A person (or more) has noticed me at work. I've been asked about my general work ethic. This is the typical stuff...

"Yo, man. What's the deal with ya? Why do you work so hard? How aren't you tired?"

I remembered the Stone Cold BMF. I was talking about it with one of my closest friends (during downtime). It got me thinking. I wound up saying the below exactly to variations:

I know where I am. There are cameras everywhere. We're being watched through the day. I notice these kids getting really lax (at times). Those same guys (or hats) don't wanna do shit.

They'll move the minute that a Process Assistant comes around. They'll kiss their ass. Once the chat is over, they'll return to what they were doing. They're even worse when an Operations Manager shows up. That's when they'll really go.

Me?

I give management no reason to fuck with me. I'm here to kick ass for nearly twelve hours (in actual time). I come in early. Not just for the money. I do it to set up for a good shift. These kids won't do it. They're not bred as I am.

You wonder why managers come to me? Why do people call me the Leader of Tote Stacker? I am always moving. I live by GSD. GSD is *Getting Shit Done*.

Back to the present time…

Let me remind you that I hear people complain about general life. The most major on their list is a lack of time. How 24 hours is not enough time to do stuff. Wishing there was more for whatever they truly loved to do.

I used to come from that same vibration. I was whining about how I couldn't record my podcast. The length of time to sleep then return to work. Not being able to write generally.

I was deep in meditation one day. I remembered the GSD. I applied it not just to my work life. I did so for years. I still do to this every day.

I made it a habit. I stopped my boo-hoo-hooing. I started seeing value in my time. Why? It is the time allotted for me.

I make the time every day. I make sure to eat throughout my day. I stay nourished with non-alcohol to mega sugary drinks. I am reading articles, blogs, books, or whatever I am interested in. I am watching stuff that brings out the GSD.

I am around people who have that GSD in them. They motivate me. I believe I fire their asses up too. I love that so much.

Having Fun

"All work and no play makes for a dull person."

As I wrap up this book, why not talk about the importance of fun. I love being focused. It brought me so much success. There are times when I'm so focused that I can zonk myself.

I recall October to November 2019. It wasn't just the end of a near-decade romance. It wasn't where I took measures to get my health together. It was really about me rebuilding myself as a person.

I wanted to reverse my diabetes? Yes, I did. Did I yearn to lose weight? Right on. There was something that my heart desired to do. That was having fun.

I knew I couldn't be physically active all the time. There would be points where I needed to rest. Giving myself time to relax was crucial for me. It allowed my body to adapt to what I did. It took pressure (especially of high blood) off my ass.

So what did I do? Remind myself of that quote I used to kick off this section. I applied every day that I could. Let my mind relax. Know that I am doing alright.

Movies and TV

I wasn't on social media from October 2019 until May 2020. It opened me up to watching TV again. I don't watch stuff with commercials. When I'm alone, I have ad-free viewings. I love to witness things fully.

The Coronavirus Pandemic limited me in different ways; however, it was an unknowing ally. I used to go crazy about going to see movies in theaters. That was one of my favorite things to do. It goes back to me being Little Zachary Shilohkins.

My dad would take me (and/or our immediate family) to see stuff like *The Nutty Professor* (starring Eddie Murphy). His older sister was the same way. She was more child-friendly (with stuff such as Disney's *The Lion King*). This would follow me my entire life.

As 2022 roared along for me, I saw the blessing of being without the movie theater. On-demand services such as Netflix and Hulu became my outlet to view whatever I wanted. I reminisced with TV shows such as *DC's Titans*, *Power Rangers Beast Morphers*, and *Wu-Tang: An American Saga*.

They showed me why I couldn't stand to go to the movie theaters. I was paying double-digit money for one show. Nearly to exact triple digits for up to four. Food was ridiculous to pay for. It's the same for popcorn, "soft" drinks, pretzels, etc.

We, human beings, are like animals. We have certain bodily functions. Unfortunately, we aren't blessed to be in the wild from sunrise to dusk. We have to practice retention throughout our days. That especially goes for being in a movie theater.

I am a person who loves to be in-depth with things. I love it when stories are told. I can feel emotions higher than others. This sucks when I have to use the bathroom. I wound up missing scenes of movies (depending on my bathroom use).

It didn't help me that I crawled over other viewers. This caused them to miss something. Bothered me even more when I had my romantic partner, a friend, or whomever with me. Really upset me having to do the reverse.

I was thinking about this as I waited for the second *Sonic the Hedgehog* film (to be in theaters). I could see the benefits of waiting for On-demand.

I didn't have to bother people while they were watching the same movie. I was saving money. If I had to relieve human nature, I was free to do so (after taking a pause). I didn't have to hear other people dubbing with commentary.

Reading

When I was a kid, it was something I loved to do. A way to be entertained is through non-moving visualization or verbalization. A form of media enjoyed in silence. I would distance myself from it by way of chapter books as I became an adult.

When I was diabetic, I didn't just yearn to watch movies and TV. I had a higher brain capacity than that. I remembered that

I loved to read. I did so by research. I'd look up geeky things (such as conventions, how-to dos, etc.).

I wanted a better relationship with books. I had an Amazon Kindle. I thought, *"Why not?"* I was social media free. So, I bought a book called *"Why Delete Your Social Media Accounts."* That would lead me to read other chapter books.

I found comic books even more appealing. I mentioned reading *Power Rangers*. A different series I loved is *Batman: The Adventures Continue*. I loved *Batman: The Animated Series* as a child. I heard that some series personnel were putting brand-new adventures into comics.

I bought some issues. Felt as if I had never stopped watching the TV show. Everything that I knew was intact. The setting is the same. The characters' dialogue could be for kids, teens, and adults.

YouTube

It's an outlet for the visual *BLK Lion's Domain*. It's been something I enjoyed before being a podcaster. I use it daily. I can be without it for about twelve hours (if I want).

YouTube is my primary source of music. I found songs I heard as a lad. People who are close to me send stuff that they like. Some stuff is enjoyable. Others are *"Are you serious?"* territory.

If I want to hear other podcasts, I will tune in. I get a couple of laughs from podcasters. I can listen to their opinions on their topics. I can feel their passion (especially if it's what they love).

Listening to whatever I want really calms me down. I can do my laundry. I can take a shower. I can go for a walk. Be in a positive mood. Feel my frequency get higher.

Writing

I really love to write. It's not just meditation. Goes beyond affirmations. I do have genuine fun with it. I sometimes do it with music going on.

I laugh at some thoughts. I smile as I reminisce. Let my inner child loose to play. Really get *"chefy,"* as a dear friend would say. I have so much fun doing this that sometimes I fall asleep.

What Zachary Shiloh Eats to Stay Under 200 Pounds

Many people want to lose weight. They ask, *"How can I lose ____?"* They go looking for answers.

As of December 10, 2022, I have been under 200 pounds over three years. I have documented most of the food I ate since November 8, 2019. I added some stuff since then. Decreased (or removed) stuff throughout the years.

I was talking to a dear friend/co-worker. He wanted to change his life a bit. Told me about his health issues. I noticed him being sluggish as the day was coming to an end. I told Heavy D (as I call the guy) that I would make a list of foods I ate.

I thought that I needed my food journal. I began with what I ate recently. My food came out one by one. I wound up stopping work at points to write them out. I was ready for my final eating time anyway. So, no real harm in production, myself and others.

Three weeks later saw me reminisce about my eating. I asked myself, *"What did I want from my food?"* I could see the 32-year-old Zachary Shiloh using one of his strengths. He is channeling the power of research.

I would research throughout my day. The location of myself didn't matter. If I could do it, then I went where I was guided.

I used downtime at the nursing home. I continued from the comfort of my home.

What did I want?

I wanted to be energized. I sought to build muscle tone. Help me to regulate my blood pressure. Knock down my depression.

The following is what I ate over the last three years that helped me stay under 200 pounds:

Almonds

Apples

Avocados

Bagels

Bananas

Beef jerky

Beef stew

Beets

Blackberries

Broccoli

Butternut squash

Cantaloupe

Cauliflower

Carrots

Chayote

Cherries

Chicken

Celery

Clams

Collard Greens

Couscous

Crackers

Cucumber

Curry beef

Curry chicken

Dragonfruit

Eggs

English Muffins

Garlic

Grapes

Green Beans

Ground Beef

Ground Chicken

Ground Lamb

Ground Pork

Ground Turkey

Flaxseeds

Ham

Hempseeds

Honeydew

Hot dogs

Jello (sugar-free)

Kale

Kiwi

Lettuce

Lintels

Melon

Mint

Nigella

Oats

Onions

Papaya

Pasta (veggie)

Peas

Pepper

Pepperoni

Persimmon

Pistachios

Popcorn

Pork chops

Potatoes

Potato chips

Pretzels

Pumpkin

Onions

Oranges

Quinoa

Raspberries

Ribs

Rice

Salmon

Salsa

Sausage

Shrimp

Squash

Starfruit

Strawberries

Sunflower Seeds

Sweet Potatoes

Tomatoes

Tortillas (flat)

Tortilla Chips

Tuna

Turkey

Turkey Jerky

Watermelon

Yogurt

Zucchini

The Forbidden

With good stuff in life, there is an alternate version. I remember my life after 2010. I own myself for the time. I don't hate myself for how I ate.

I wasn't eating right. I was a very picky eater. I really disregarded the nutritional facts. I was surrounded by people who didn't take care of themselves well (since childhood).

What I was consuming on a daily basis wasn't because I was completely hungry. I was in pain. I was emotionally, financially, mentally, physically, and spiritually hurting. I was able to vent to food more than people I loved.

These things didn't judge me. They smelled good to me. They made me believe that life was more positive with them around me. They proved me wrong timed again. They made me completely blind to the truth.

They pissed me off more. I wasn't full from the consumption. I was urinating dark. I was grabbing at my heart at times. I felt someone choking the life out of me.

As of 2019, I forgot my name was Zachary Shiloh Watts. I was forgetting not just my name. I was losing the memory of my loved ones. I didn't know what year I was in. I couldn't recall where I was from. I was lucky to know my age.

My problems kept building. I couldn't sleep at times. My anxiety kicked my ass. Once I learned about what I was eating, I decided to stop eating the following.

Biscuits

Breaded chicken

Breaded shrimp

Brownies

Cake

Cheerios

Chips Ahoy

Cinnamon Buns

Cinnamon Toast Crunch

Coffee Cake

Cookie Crisps

Cornbread

Donuts

French Toast Sticks

Fried Chicken

Fried Fish

Fried Oreos

Frosted Flakes

Frosting

Granola

Italian Ices

Juju Coins

Lucky Charms

Marshmallows

Pancakes

Pie

Rice Krispies

Starburst

Swedish Fish

Sweet Potato pie

Sugar

Tropical Skittles

Tropical Starbursts

Twizzlers

Waffles

Water Taffy

Zeppoles

None of the above help me to live my life. They plagued me for many years. It's been quite a world without them. I have no regrets.

What makes me keep away from The Forbidden?

It's not just my memories. I feel what they did to me still. I see what they're doing to people around this beautiful planet. If it's not building the human race, I want no part of it.

The Untouchables

Accessories can go good with some things. A purse can work with a woman who wears a dress. A tie can add presence to a man's suit. People are complimented for their choices to use these items. These decisions are so impactful that folks still buzz positively days later.

What if this isn't just with clothing? What if the food you eat can have an accessory (or more)? What if the stuff you drink adds to what you eat?

This happened to me… It's followed me for many years, too. One thing really showed itself. I'm happy and grateful for some laws. I understand better as an adult (in his 30s).

Some other items didn't hit me until 2019. I was an oblivious durp. I grew up believing they went well with what I ate. Their consumption wouldn't harm me.

How they look deceived me. Their existence plagued my life. Their taste was like cocaine. I desired them morning, noon, and night. I was a dedicated junkie.

They were stabbing me in the heart. They were killing my cells daily. The weight they gave me felt like overlaying concrete over time.

These mobsters had no code of honor. It was their way or the highway. Messed with one, then you were sleeping with these fishes.

These hoodlums thought they'd rule forever. That they would not be opposed. Everyone would be their loyal pets. Mighty historical figures had this mentality. They were absolutely wrong.

Adolf Hitler's reign over Germany ended. Julius Caesar's domination of Rome was ceased. Al Capone's hold on New York City was stopped. Joseph Stalin's demonic gripe on Russia was halted. Mao Zedong's hand on China was removed.

These punks were destroying my life. Their influence wasn't only impacting me. They were brainwashing my family. They affected generations of other human beings.

They forced me to change. To look at how relationships have, are, and will implode. Why people are on excessive medications. How individuals were, have, and continue gaining weight.

These are the smooth criminals that longer have any hold on me:

Arizona teas

Beer

Big Burst

Coca Cola

Cream Soda

Fanta

Gatorade

Ginger Ale

Hawaiian Punch

Juicy Juice

Minute Maid

Mountain Dew

Pepsi

Pina Colada

Root Beer

Slushies

Sunkist

Sunny D

Tropical Fantasy

This liberated man hasn't yearned to be enslaved again. He knows the price of true freedom. Feels damn good to not be a hostage.

Where Am I Now

When you are reading this, I have to believe it is near the end of 2023. I am going to be honest. It's not just a Bon Jovi song, but *I'm living on a prayer*. With tears flowing out of my eyes, I am praying the Serenity Prayer, to be exact.

I am still staying consistent with what made me successful. What I do isn't a weekly thing. It's not bi to full monthly. It's not yearly. I continue going every day.

I have spoken at the *Step into Your Magic* summit (hosted by Blair Hayse). It is my first virtual summit in years. I have left people a mini guide on how to roar towards their dreams.

I have been off fast-food for over a year with two restaurants by me. The fast-food accomplishment continues years of non-fast-food across the island I am on.

My podcast is roaring louder than it has ever been. I am doing episodes weekly. I am getting ready to crack 10,000 plays wherever I am here. I am interviewing people I have known from mere days to years in the Uncensored Plateau, where Universal Ground is partaken. Reaching a feat, I think seldom human beings have reached called Season Five.

I have no co-authoring releases this year. It's funny for me to say that. When I am writing this section, I can see the last two years. I had a release for every February since 2021. February 2023 is the first time I am resting.

I have invested in unsung self-developers. I am channeling my creativity stronger. I am beginning to follow up this book.

Outro

As I wrap up this book completely, this is the part that I struggled with the most. I wanted to end with something flashy. I honestly did, kids out there.

I wanted to add more to this book. My other co-authoring journeys I had (beyond the eight that I recognized). Things that I have added to my life since 2022. As all of this hit me, it dawned on what this book was about initially.

What this book evolved into was more than what I expected. I gave my life to you in multidimensional ways. I shared eight powerful co-authoring journeys. You traveled with me from late 2019 through early 2023. You experienced some of my most rough times.

I am sure you had some laughs. There must have been some tears shed (or yearning to do so). I believe that you're taking away some things of value.

You may have more courage to endure building a business. You can be proud to be a geek (like I am). Take action to write your own solo book. Want to join someone like Blair Hayse, DarkQuarks Publishing, or Melissa Desveaux in their writing anthology series. Heck, you may want to do your own co-authoring.

I know I did this before the introduction, but I say thank you (once again). There is a chance we know each other. You could have known me since we were in proper childhood. Our paths crossed as adults.

If we have never met, this really means a lot to me. You read about a complete stranger. May feel the pull to be part of my life (beyond this). I still am grateful, even if this was a one-time deal.

This book was made from one true goal. One undisputed aim. One pure focus. One undeniable track. That is lovins.

Even if I was venting, there is something I have. That is passion. I am passionate about my general writing. I am dedicated to my podcast (even if I have spent days to weeks without recordings). I love everyone I mentioned by name (even if they're out of my life in any form, shape, or whatever).

I want to leave this world better than I was born into it. If this book has helped anyone in some way, I feel blessed. Means more than money. That has a stronger value than gold.

Someone once said to me, *"What you do is bullshit."* I never forgot it. I will always remember that memory. It fuels me, not just for myself.

I ask you to know that you are not alone. You are loved. You are seen. You are heard. You are felt. You are known somehow.

You don't need a government to feel valuable. You don't need celebrity status. You have power. You are smart. You are gorgeous (even you goofball men, too).

About the Author

Zachary Shiloh Watts is an all-life New Yorker. He was born in Brooklyn, NY (during the winter of 1987). Has resided in Staten Island (since 1997). He is the proud middle of three children.

His favorite season is Spring. His favorite color is red. When talking with Zach, he tends to not cuss. Should he curse, then it goes with what he is conveying (at the time). He loves being in nature. Weight trains 3X a week.

When he isn't working, Zach is pursuing his wildest dreams. One of them happens to be his love of writing. He has the honor of saying he is a Best-Selling Author.

Another passion is the expansion of what he calls BLK Lion's Airspace. BLK Lion's Airspace is the Flowtastic Zone where LOVE shines brightest. Home of the BLK Lion's Domain interview segment (where Universal Grounding is partaken). He discusses Universal Laws (more so the Law of Attraction), writing, health, and whatever else keeps him highly vibrational. His podcast has been around since June 16, 2019.

Please contact and support Zachary Shiloh by using the following links:

https://www.facebook.com/BLKLion130/

https://twitter.com/BLKLion130

https://www.instagram.com/blklion130/

www.ingramcontent.com/pod-product-compliance
Lightning Source LLC
LaVergne TN
LVHW010215070526
838199LV00062B/4600